# THE COMPLETE GUIDE TO
# spinning yarn

# THE COMPLETE GUIDE TO
# spinning yarn

## TECHNIQUES, PROJECTS, AND RECIPES

### BRENDA GIBSON

St. Martin's Griffin
New York

The Complete Guide to Spinning Yarn
Copyright © 2011 by Quarto Inc.

www.stmartins.com

Library of Congress Cataloguing-in-Publication
data available upon request.

ISBN: 978-0-312-59138-0

First U.S. edition: January 2012

Conceived, designed, and produced by
Quarto Publishing plc
The Old Brewery
6 Blundell Street
London N7 9BH

QUAR.SPIN

Senior editor: Chloe Todd Fordham
Assistant art editor: Kate Bramley
Designer: Kieran Stevens
Illustrator: Kuo Kang Chen
Consultant: Eling Chang
Photographer: Simon Pask
Art director: Caroline Guest
Creative director: Moira Clinch
Publisher: Paul Carslake

Color separation in Singapore by
PICA Digital Pte Ltd
Printed in Singapore by
Star Standard Industries (PTE) Ltd

10 9 8 7 6 5 4 3 2 1

# Contents

| | |
|---|---|
| Author's foreword | 6 |
| About this book | 6 |
| **Chapter 1: Foundations** | **8** |
| A brief history of spinning | 10 |
| Fiber preparation tools | 14 |
| Spindles | 16 |
| Wheels | 18 |
| Plying and yarn handling tools | 22 |
| Fibers | 24 |
| **Chapter 2: Techniques** | **28** |
| Scouring | 30 |
| Teasing | 31 |
| Carding | 32 |
| Blending | 34 |
| Making rolags and punis | 36 |

| | | | | |
|---|---|---|---|---|
| Pre-drafting | 38 | | Spiral thick and thin yarn | 86 |
| Combing | 40 | | Cable-plied yarn | 88 |
| Dyeing | 42 | | Color-blended yarn | 90 |
| Spindle spinning | 46 | | Flecked yarn | 92 |
| Wheel spinning | 50 | | Slub yarn | 94 |
| Worsted spinning | 54 | | Three-ply chunky yarn | 96 |
| Woolen spinning | 56 | | Chain-plied color yarn | 98 |
| Spinning from the fold | 58 | | Core-spun yarn | 100 |
| Direction and balance | 59 | | Bouclé yarn | 102 |
| Thick and thin spinning | 60 | | Paper yarn | 104 |
| Spinning for evenness or texture | 62 | | Bullion yarn | 106 |
| Conventional plying | 64 | | | |
| Navajo or chain plying | 67 | | **Chapter 4: Projects** | **108** |
| Andean plying | 68 | | Woven pillow cover | 110 |
| Fancy yarn plying | 70 | | Knitted hat and mittens | 112 |
| Making a skein | 74 | | Tassels | 117 |
| Blocking | 76 | | Knitted slipcase | 120 |
| Washing and finishing | 77 | | | |
| Winding balls | 78 | | **Chapter 5:** | |
| | | | **Professional approaches** | **122** |
| **Chapter 3: Recipes** | **80** | | Going commercial | 124 |
| Soft knitting yarn | 82 | | Planning and record-keeping | 132 |
| Lustrous worsted yarn | 84 | | Gallery | 134 |
| | | | | |
| | | | Health and safety | 140 |
| | | | Glossary | 141 |
| | | | Index | 143 |
| | | | Credits | 144 |

# Author's foreword

I owe a great deal to a chance encounter with the art of spinning over 25 years ago. It prompted me to learn a new skill that has not been a passing whim but has led me in new and exciting textile directions, has introduced me to many good friends, and has been a constant source of anti-stress therapy. I hope this book will take you on a similar journey of discovery.

This book encompasses a wide range of techniques and ideas. It is highly accessible to beginners, but aims to be a continuing creative stimulus and source of reference for intermediate and experienced spinners, too.

Brenda Gibson

### Left- or right-handed?
Throughout this book, instructions and photography are written by a right-handed person and show the left and right hands in a particular orientation. You may be comfortable following the instructions exactly as given, but, irrespective of whether you are right- or left-handed, it is worth reversing the hands and trying the action the other way round to see if that feels more comfortable and natural. When it comes to spinning actions, there seems to be no clear right or wrong way round for left- and right-handed people.

# About this book

Whether you are a beginner or an experienced spinner, this book will teach you everything you need to know to make and utilize beautiful homespun yarn. The book is organized into five key chapters that take you through this varied and versatile craft, from purchasing your first spinning wheel to professional approaches such as marketing and pricing your projects.

### Chapter one:
## Foundations (pages 8–27)
Before you take to the wheel, you will need to make sure you have the right tools for the job. Whether it is spinning wheels, spindles, yarn handling tools, fiber, or fiber preparation tools, this chapter will ensure you have everything you need to get started.

### Chapter two:
## Techniques (pages 28–79)
Step-by-step sequences explain techniques for the preparation of fibers, spinning a single thread, plying single threads together to make a balanced yarn, creative use of color, and much more.

### Chapter three:
## Recipes (pages 80–107)
Once you have mastered the techniques in chapter two, try your hand at the recipes. In this chapter you will see featured a huge range of exquisite, textured yarns in single or mixed colorways—from subtly sensuous mohairs to crisp two-plies and the lovely nubbly charms of flecked, spiral, bouclé, and bullion yarns.

### Chapter four:
## Projects (pages 108–121)
Now, put your skills into action. Whether you prefer knitting, weaving, or crochet, these basic projects are sure to show off your handspun yarns. Knit a hat and mittens, weave a pillow cover, make a slipcase for a notebook, or adorn your home with some decorative tassels.

### Chapter five:
## Professional approaches (pages 122–139)
From collaborating with other spinners, knitters, and crocheters, building your own website and promoting your own work, to finding and accepting commissions and demonstrating at craft fairs, this unique chapter tells you all you need to know to go pro. Experience the sort of work professional spinners are making in the six-page gallery section starting on page 134, and get spinning.

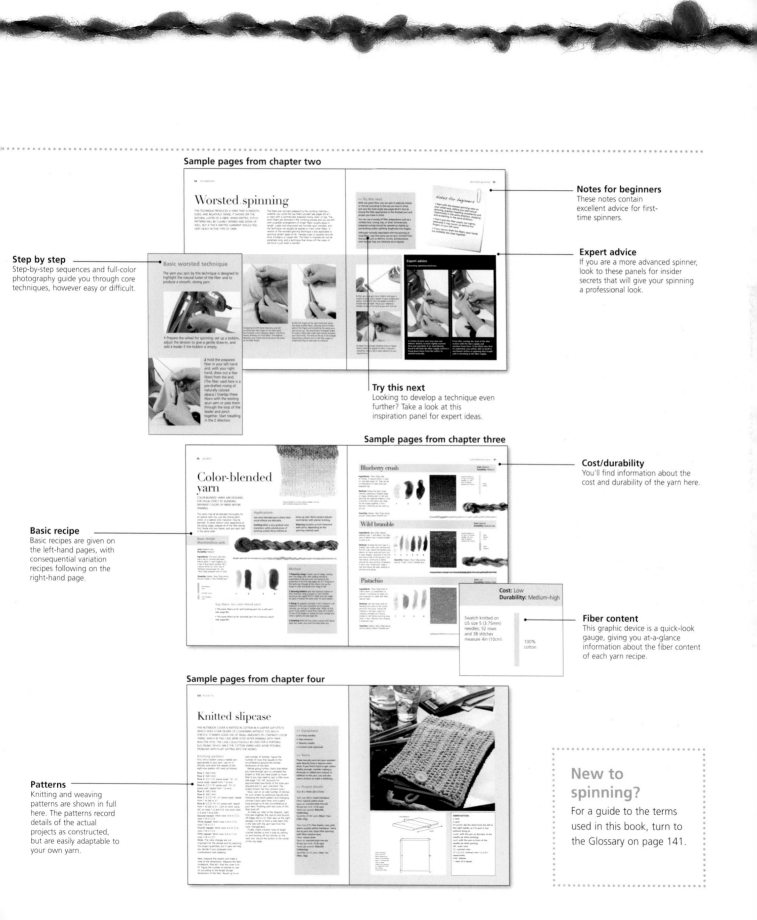

## Sample pages from chapter two

**Notes for beginners**
These notes contain excellent advice for first-time spinners.

**Expert advice**
If you are a more advanced spinner, look to these panels for insider secrets that will give your spinning a professional look.

**Step by step**
Step-by-step sequences and full-color photography guide you through core techniques, however easy or difficult.

**Try this next**
Looking to develop a technique even further? Take a look at this inspiration panel for expert ideas.

## Sample pages from chapter three

**Cost/durability**
You'll find information about the cost and durability of the yarn here.

**Basic recipe**
Basic recipes are given on the left-hand pages, with consequential variation recipes following on the right-hand page.

**Fiber content**
This graphic device is a quick-look gauge, giving you at-a-glance information about the fiber content of each yarn recipe.

## Sample pages from chapter four

**Patterns**
Knitting and weaving patterns are shown in full here. The patterns record details of the actual projects as constructed, but are easily adaptable to your own yarn.

## New to spinning?

For a guide to the terms used in this book, turn to the Glossary on page 141.

*Chapter 1*

# Foundations

*This chapter introduces you to the ancient origins of spinning, the tools of the trade, and the huge variety of fibers from which you can create wonderful yarns. By understanding the purpose of the various tools and fibers, you can decide how to prioritize purchases and get started with spinning.*

# A brief history of spinning

THE EARLIEST FIND OF SPUN FIBER (IN THE FORM OF STRING OR ROPE) MAY HAVE COME FROM ISRAEL AND DATES FROM AROUND 17,000 YEARS AGO. TEXTILES DO NOT WITHSTAND THE RAVAGES OF TIME EASILY, LIKE STONE OR METAL ARTIFACTS, BUT THERE ARE MANY EARLY EXAMPLES OF EVIDENCE OF CORDAGE BECAUSE IMPRESSIONS ARE SO OFTEN FOUND IN POTTERY.

The earliest finds of actual string in the USA (at the Cave of the Chimneys on San Miguel Island) and in the UK (at a submerged hunter-gatherer camp off the coast of the Isle of Wight) both date from around 8,000 years ago. The construction of primitive yarns predates archaeological finds of spindle whorls; these were made using a thigh-spinning technique. Holding one end of some fiber (such as grass) in one hand, it can be rolled up the thigh with the palm of the other hand to impart a twist. Two separate strands can be twisted in this way and then both rolled back together in the opposite direction to create a plied yarn with absolutely no equipment!

## Spindle whorls

The British Museum has in its collection a spindle whorl dating from 6000–5000 BCE, evidence of spinning using hand spindles. It was excavated at Tell Arpachiyah, an Ancient Near East prehistoric site about 4 miles (6.5km) from Nineveh (outside modern Mosul in Iraq). Spindle whorls and loom weights (they cannot necessarily be distinguished) are common later archaeological finds, though the wooden spindles have usually perished. The transition to spinning using spindles rather than the cruder thigh-spinning process would have marked a step-change in the rate of yarn production and would have enabled fine results to be achieved in skillful hands.

## Spindle wheels

Spinning wheels are a much more recent development; some types of wheel are believed to have been known in India and China from between 500 and 1000 CE. The earliest type of wheel would have been a simple mechanization of a spindle, and would still have involved the separation of the process of adding twist from that of storing the spun yarn on the spindle. There would have been no treadle and no flyer. The advantage of this type of wheel over a spindle was the ease with which the spindle could be rotated at high speed, due to the gearing effect of driving from a large-diameter wheel to a small-diameter spindle. Spinning wheels were not commonplace elsewhere in the world for a long time; the hand spindle was still ubiquitous and it is likely that the linen sails for the ships of the great explorers were made from spindle-spun linen.

Spindle wheels vary in size and style—from the Great Wheel to the charkha. The Great Wheel, also known as the Walking Wheel, was normally used for the spinning of wool. It features a very large-diameter wheel driving an exposed spindle, onto which the spinner would woolen-spin using a one-handed long-draw technique. With one hand employed in driving the wheel, long-draw spinning is very necessary.

Cotton spinning was important in India, and the high twist ratio of the hand-powered charkha wheel (which is a variation with further gearing from large to small diameters) makes it an ideal tool for the job.

Mahatma Gandhi was a great proponent of the benefits to the rural economy of India of hand spinning cotton using the charkha, and the charkha appeared on the flag of the Provisional Government of Free India.

### GREAT WHEEL
The spinner's right hand rotates the wheel as she drafts from the rolag using her left hand, adding twist from the point of the spindle. A cop of spun yarn can be seen on the spindle.

**ST ELIZABETH OF HUNGARY SPINNING FOR THE POOR**
This oil painting, by Marianne Stokes in 1895, depicts St Elizabeth spinning using a treadle and flyer wheel of a design then popular in Europe. She is spinning wool from a distaff. However, as St Elizabeth was canonized in 1235, pre-dating this type of wheel by several centuries, artistic license has been used.

**MAHATMA GANDHI**
Mahatma Gandhi seated peacefully before a traditional charkha. Gandhi encouraged everyone to spin a little every day, for spiritual as well as for economic reasons.

## Spinning in fairy tales

As spinning was so very much a part of everyday household life before the industrial revolution, it should come as no surprise that spinning is referenced in several fairy tales. One of the most well known is the tale of Sleeping Beauty. In fact, the most popular question from small children who see spinning is where on the wheel she pricked her finger. The wheel in the fairy tale would have been a spindle wheel, which does have an exposed sharp point, though similar hazards are absent from modern flyer-based wheels—much to the childrens' usual disappointment. Another well-known tale is that of Rumpelstiltskin (right), where a miller falsely claimed that his daughter could spin straw into gold to gain the attention of the king; the gnome Rumpelstiltskin could actually do so and was thereby able to extract bribes. This tale must surely relate to the spinning of flax, which looks for all the world like a bundle of unpromising straw in its raw state, but yields beautiful fine gold-colored fibers after being hackled ready for spinning.

## Flyer and treadle

Moving on from the spindle wheel, the next significant developments were the advent of the flyer and treadle, both in the 16th century. The impact of the flyer was to create a continuous process whereby the spun yarn would wind onto the bobbin automatically without the need to interrupt the flow of spinning to wind on manually. The impact of the treadle was to free up both hands, so enabling a short-draw technique to be used, as well as to help speed up the process. Taken together, these two developments would have greatly increased spinning productivity. These wheels would soon start to look very familiar to present-day spinners.

## Mechanization

Mechanization of the spinning process was an important aspect of the industrial revolution in England, with the invention of large-scale carding machines, the Spinning Jenny (a multi-spool spinning frame invented around 1764) and larger scale water-powered frames patented by Richard Arkwright, who earned enormous riches from his textile mill activities.

Samuel Slater, who had been raised in England and apprenticed in a spinning mill, emigrated to America in 1789 at a time when the Quaker patron Moses Brown was dependent on English equipment for spinning thread. After

they discovered each other, Slater went on to design new homegrown American-equipped mills based on his knowledge of the Arkwright model. The Brown–Slater partnership was hugely successful, and also involved Slater's wife Hannah, (the daughter of Moses Brown's business partner). Hannah Slater became the first woman to file for an American patent for a new way to spin thread.

## Modern spinning

From this point on, the domestic and industrial spinning processes diverged quite markedly. Most present-day industrial spinning uses either ring-spinning or air-jet systems to create vast quantities of yarn at high speed with minimal manual intervention. But the present-day craft of hand spinning continues to innovate in wheel and spindle design. There are electric spinners on the market; as well as enabling a high rate of spinning production they can be a great boon for disabled people. In a world where living space is at a premium, folding wheels are now very popular, and are very useful for taking out and about to events such as spinning demonstrations and guild meetings. Double-treadle wheels are also very widely manufactured these days—they are almost the default option for a new wheel—and make for a very smooth and regular treadling motion that's kind on the body, provided that you sit square to the wheel.

So in 17,000 or so years, we have come quite a long way, and yet there is still a strong link to the technology of the past. It's wonderful to look in a museum case at a spindle whorl and know exactly how to pick it up, push a stick through it, and spin a totally 21st-century yarn with a very ancient tool.

**SPINNING JENNY**
Invented around 1764, this machine could spin multiple spindles of cotton simultaneously, using a long-draw technique.

**RUMPELSTILTSKIN**
In this fairy tale, Rumpelstiltskin helped save the life of a miller's daughter by "spinning straw into gold." This was clearly a reference to the spinning of flax, which is a natural golden color and capable of being spun into a very fine yarn.

**MULE SPINNING MACHINE**
Invented in the late 1770s by Samuel Crompton, this machine also uses the long-draw technique to spin a large number of spindles simultaneously. It was the most popular spinning machine until about 1900, with some rare examples still in use today.

**MODERN TEXTILE PRODUCTION**
Modern spinning machinery requires very little human intervention and is based on a continuous flyer-based process rather than the two distinct stages (spinning yarn then storing it) of earlier methods.

# Fiber preparation tools

FIBER PREPARATION TOOLS ENABLE YOU TO START OUT WITH RAW FIBER, SUCH AS FLEECE STRAIGHT FROM THE ANIMAL'S BACK, AND CREATE A PREPARATION SUCH AS A ROLAG, PUNI, OR ROVING FROM WHICH YOU CAN SPIN DIRECTLY.

Different tools are appropriate to different fibers. The specialized tools required for long-bast fibers (flax etc.) are beyond the scope of this book and are omitted. Many of the tools you will need are quite simple and inexpensive; some are more specialized and optional, at least to start with. Different tools may also relate to different preparations of the same fiber—wool may be prepared by carding for woolen spinning or by combing for worsted spinning, for example (see pages 54–57).

Scouring (washing out the grease) is part of preparation for some fibers too, and it's useful to have a standard domestic mesh laundry bag for controlling the loose fiber.

As a beginner, you will want a dog comb as a minimum. This will enable you to comb a lock of fleece and spin a lovely worsted-type yarn from it. Some tools for carding will be your next priority, and a pair of hand carders is a must, even if you have a drum carder. Carders have different grades of carding cloth, and a fine luxury fiber does need to be matched with a fine grade of carding cloth for good results. For combing, in addition to a dog comb, a pair of mini combs can be very useful. These are ideal for creating a roving from fine fibers; they are

light, portable, and not too expensive. Carders and combs are both used for blending—fibers and colors—according to the spinning preparation you require, so are a very relevant part of your equipment even if you will mostly spin from ready-prepared fibers.

The "big boys" of fiber preparation are the drum carder for woolen-style batts and English wool combs for worsted-style rovings. A drum carder makes light work of large quantities of fiber, and is very useful if you will be processing whole fleece. A set of English wool combs is the tool of choice for processing quantities of uniform rovings with all the short fibers removed. Both of these items are a major personal investment but can sometimes be borrowed from a spinning guild.

These smaller, curved hand carders are designed for carding cotton. Their fine teeth make them very suitable for other fine fibers such as cashmere, angora, and silk.

✿ Indicates tools recommended for beginners to try first.

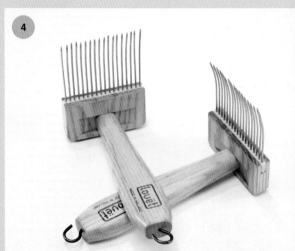

### 1 HAND CARDERS ✪
Hand carders are available with either flat or curved backs, and with different grades of carding cloth. Choose a medium grade to start with. If you can, try them out before you buy to see which type feels more comfortable for you to use. Cotton carders are a little smaller and with finer cloth—they are ideal for silk too.

### 2 DOG COMBS ✪
These simple combs can be bought from a pet store as well as from specialized fiber suppliers. You need the strength of a comb with metal teeth rather than a hair comb.

### 3 FLICK CARDER
This small carding device is used singly rather than as part of a pair. Like a dog comb, it is used with a tapping motion onto a leather or sturdy fabric pad on your lap.

### 4 MINI COMBS
Mini combs are used in pairs and are available with either single or multiple rows of tines. Multiple tines hold the fibers more securely but cost more than the single-tine equivalent. The tines are extremely sharp so, for transport purposes, keep them in their original box or make special protectors for the very sharp points.

### 5 DRUM CARDER
As with hand carders, the grade of card clothing must relate to the type of end use you have in mind, though a medium grade will suit most purposes. Most are hand cranked, but some electric versions are available. Make sure you can adjust the alignment of the drums so that the tines are not touching but are only the thickness of a sheet of paper apart. The metal rod, known as the doffer, is used to remove the carded batt from the large drum.

# Spindles

MODERN SPINDLES ARE BEAUTIFULLY MADE, IMPECCABLY BALANCED, AND ARE A JOY TO USE. THEY COME IN DIFFERENT WEIGHTS, ACCORDING TO THE THICKNESS OF YARN YOU WANT TO SPIN, AND IN DIFFERENT SHAPES—THE COUNTER-INTUITIVE SQUARE WHORL IS BECOMING INCREASINGLY POPULAR AND SPINS BEAUTIFULLY.

The whorl may be at the top, bottom, or (rarely) even in the middle, and the shaft may have a notch or a hook. If you grow to love spindle spinning, collecting spindles can become quite addictive—you have been warned!

The essential quality of a spindle is that it is very well balanced, otherwise it will wobble rather than rotate smoothly and it will quickly come to a halt. The overall weight of the spindle needs to match the thickness (perhaps also the fiber) of the yarn you want to spin. A thick, strong yarn needs a heavier weight to give sufficient spinning tension and rotational energy. A lace weight yarn, on the other hand, needs a lightweight spindle, but one that will rotate a long time before stopping, since a fine yarn would break with too heavy a weight pulling on it during the spinning process and it will need a lot of twist.

The ability to maintain rotational momentum relates to a combination of weight and diameter, and it's desirable to have weight that is concentrated at the rim. This factor helps explain why square whorls can spin so well.

A spindle's capacity is also related to its overall weight, because yarn that is spun and stored on the spindle adds to that weight. The effective capacity of a heavier spindle is, therefore, greater than a lighter one.

Whenever possible, try out a spindle before buying, using a little of the fiber you wish to spin with it.

## Top-whorl spindles (1–8)

These spindles all have a hook of some sort on the short part of the shaft that passes through the whorl. They frequently also have a yarn location groove on the edge of the whorl.

**1** Basic medium-weight spindle with short shaft.

**2+3** Decorative medium-weight spindles.

**4** Medium-heavy-weight spindle, with a small diameter whorl.

## Bottom-whorl spindles (9-11)

These spindles may have either a notch or a hook at the end of the shaft away from the whorl. But as the yarn can be secured to the shaft with a half-hitch knot, some bottom whorl spindles have neither.

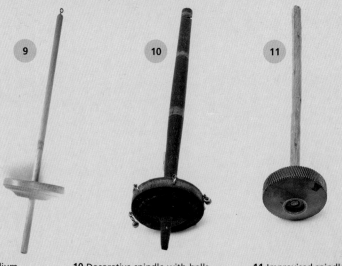

**9** Basic medium-heavy-weight spindle with top hook.

**10** Decorative spindle with bells from Nepal.

**11** Improvised spindle from Afghanistan, made of a metal gear wheel on a wooden shaft.

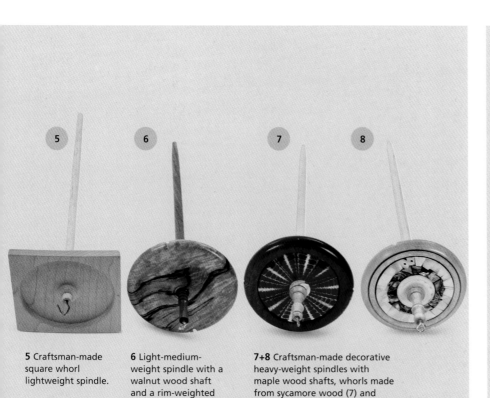

**5** Craftsman-made square whorl lightweight spindle.

**6** Light-medium-weight spindle with a walnut wood shaft and a rim-weighted whorl made of sycamore wood.

**7+8** Craftsman-made decorative heavy-weight spindles with maple wood shafts, whorls made from sycamore wood (7) and walnut wood (8), both with mosaic shell inlay.

## Specialist spindles (12–15)

Spindles come in all shapes and sizes. Supported spindles (12–14) are very lightweight spindles used for spinning cotton or cashmere. In contrast to a drop-spindle, which hangs under its own weight, a supported spindle is used resting on a surface or in a small bowl.

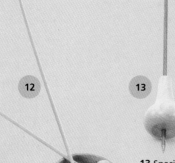

**12** Pair of bead spindles with a typical spindle bowl.

**13** Specialist spindle known as a takhli, designed to spin fast and for a long time.

**14** Simple supported spindle with a bead whorl.

**15** This specialized Turkish spindle is designed for winding the yarn round the four arms as a ball rather than winding a conventional cop round the shaft. Wind over two arms and under one, or vice versa, but not just over one under one. Slide the finished ball up and off the shaft—the cross arms will come with it. Slide the cross-arms individually out of the released ball.

## Anatomy of a spindle

The spindle shown here is a typical top-whorl spindle.

**1 SHAFT**
The shaft must be true and straight. It should be long enough to allow space for the bottom of the shaft to be rolled on the thigh or twirled in the fingers to set the spindle in motion.

**2 WHORL**
The weight and design of the whorl provides the spinning momentum of the spindle as well as tension on the yarn. The whorl must be well-balanced on the shaft so that the spindle spins true.

**3 HOOK**
The hook may be a simple curved hook or a swan-neck design. The hook must be properly centered on the shaft so that the spindle spins true.

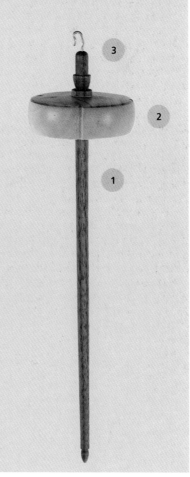

# Wheels

MODERN SPINNING WHEELS HAVE EVOLVED ELEGANTLY TO FIT IN WITH A 21ST-CENTURY LIFESTYLE, WITH SIZE, PORTABILITY, FLEXIBILITY, AND ERGONOMICS BEING IMPORTANT CONSIDERATIONS.

A simple treadle wheel will have just one treadle and may have only one spinning ratio, but will enable a variety of yarns to be produced. A more sophisticated wheel will have a range of spinning ratios to choose from—from a high ratio for fine spinning to a low ratio for thick yarns. It may also have the increasingly popular double treadle, so that you sit squarely facing the wheel and use both feet. All wheels permit tension adjustments so that you can regulate takeup, but there are technical differences to the way this is achieved, such as a double drive-band system, or scotch tension. If space is at a premium, many modern wheels are designed to fold, making them easy to transport and store.

When choosing a modern conventional flyer wheel, ask around among your friends and equipment suppliers for recommendations and, if at all possible, try before you buy. There's quite a price variation between budget models and top-of-the-range wheels, and a new wheel is a significant investment.

Some manufacturers offer specialized wheels or adaptations for spinning very fine yarns (lace flyer) or for very chunky and art yarns (jumbo flyer) where a low ratio and large orifice are a must. Some flyer designs avoid a conventional orifice altogether and have a V-shaped guide instead—these accommodate thick yarns and are very easy to thread. Some flyers also have a sliding yarn guide in place of the more conventional hooks, a well-liked feature.

## Notes for beginners

There's a thriving secondhand market, so you may be able to pick up an older wheel at a reasonable price. Beware of buying wheels from antique dealers—they are often incomplete or non-functional, and extra bobbins have to be custom-made.

## Traditional Ashford

Sloping bed traditional wheel from Ashford, one of the world's most popular manufacturers based in New Zealand. Scotch tension system, normally with single treadle, but double treadle conversion kits available if preferred.
**Advantages:** Simple, inexpensive, popular wheel; Ashford bobbins generally all interchangeable; traditional looks; widely available and options of adaptations for lace or jumbo flyer systems.
**Disadvantages:** Doesn't fold, may have a single spinning ratio, no space for bobbin storage or built-in lazy kate, scotch tension only.

## Ashford Joy

One of the earliest and most popular folding wheel designs; double treadle version (also available with single treadle).
**Advantages:** Bobbins interchangeable with other Ashfords, good range of spinning ratios, carry bag available, widely available.
**Disadvantages:** Can't be adapted for lace or jumbo flyers, not particularly small or light when folded, scotch tension only.

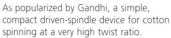

## Great Wheel

The Great Wheel (right) is the type of wheel Sleeping Beauty would have pricked her finger on. It is on the opposite end of the scale in spindle spinning terms from the charkha (above right), but operates on a similar principle.

**Advantages:** An amazing "statement piece" to have on view in your living area, the versatility of spinning from the point of a spindle, no limitation on thickness of yarn that can be spun.

**Disadvantages:** Expensive, specialized, delicate, non-portable.

## Book charkha

As popularized by Gandhi, a simple, compact driven-spindle device for cotton spinning at a very high twist ratio.

**Advantages:** Low cost, low tech, very small space required, ideal for cotton, may have built-in skein winder, a quirky conversation piece.

**Disadvantages:** Not suitable for more general spinning, requires skill in one-handed long-draw technique to use successfully, may not be widely available (imported from India).

## Lendrum wheel

This Canadian wheel with double treadle also folds for storage or transportation.

**Advantages:** Smooth and well-balanced, sliding yarn guide instead of hooks on the flyer, choice of spinning ratios.

**Disadvantages:** Not particularly small or light when folded.

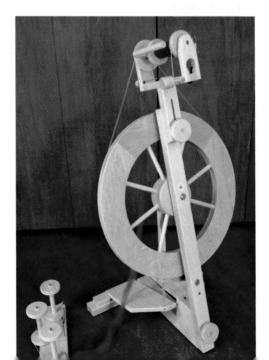

## Schacht Sidekick folding wheel

This double-treadle wheel folds in a different way due to the orientation of the drive wheel.

**Advantages:** Good choice of spinning ratios, compact and lightweight, bulky flyer option.

**Disadvantages:** Requires self-assembly.

# Anatomy of a typical wheel

The wheels shown here are contemporary treadle-operated flyer wheels. While all wheels differ in their detail, they will serve to show you the main parts and their names, and explain their functions and how the adjustments work. Some new wheels are supplied flat-packed for self-assembly. Follow the manufacturer's instructions carefully for setting up the wheel and the order in which the parts are to be assembled. Take note also of which bearings should be oiled and if there are any that must not be oiled. Oiling a wheel correctly is key to a smooth and enjoyable spinning experience.

The parts are numbered and labeled in order, starting with the action of the foot on the treadle and ending with the spun yarn.

Schacht Sidekick folding wheel shown in its operational position. Unusually, the drive wheel rotates in line with the spinner.

**1 TREADLE**
The foot presses down rhythmically once with each revolution of the wheel so that the force drives the wheel consistently in the same direction—clockwise or counterclockwise. Where the wheel design allows it, keep the pivot point of the treadle under the arch of the foot so that the wheel can be started hands-free in either direction by pressing with either the toe or the heel as appropriate. With two treadles, press each foot alternately and start hands-free using the appropriate foot.

**2 FOOTMAN**
This is the connecting shaft from each treadle to the crank connected to the axle of the main drive wheel.

**3 DRIVE WHEEL**
The wheel needs momentum to maintain smooth spinning; traditionally this was achieved using a large-diameter wheel, but smaller wheels compensate by the heavier mass of a thicker rim.

**4 DRIVE BAND**
The band extends around the drive wheel and the whorl driving either the bobbin or the flyer. A double drive band is a double-length band that extends once around the drive wheel and the bobbin whorl, around the drive wheel a second time, and around the flyer whorl.

**5 FLYER WHORL**
The grooved disk mounted on the same axle as the bobbin around which the drive band passes. Different grooves of varying diameters relate to different spinning ratios that can be selected—the smaller the diameter, the faster the spinning ratio.

**6 DRIVE BAND TENSION ADJUSTER**
On traditional wheels, a wooden screw adjusts the distance between the drive wheel and the whorl being driven. Feel the tension with your hand—it should be neither drum-tight nor loose. As you treadle, the drive band must not slip on the whorl. Note that many modern wheels employ a flexible drive band, so there is no provision for separate adjustment of drive-band tension.

**7 BRAKE TENSION ADJUSTER**
On scotch tension systems, a brake band passes over a groove in the bobbin and is tensioned by a spring. Adjust the tension while treadling with a leader on the bobbin until the pull-in of the yarn is easy to resist but takes up readily on the bobbin when released. Note that there is no separate brake tension adjuster with a double drive band.

**8 BOBBIN**
The bobbin collects the spun yarn under a little tension and is removable. A wheel will normally need at least three bobbins to make 2-ply yarn. It's wise to buy spare bobbins when buying a new wheel.

**9 FLYER**
This is the U-shaped device that rotates with hooks or a yarn guide. It puts twist into the yarn when the yarn is held back, and winds the yarn onto the bobbin when the yarn is allowed to draw in. Moving from hook to hook or shifting the yarn guide position is a manual operation.

**10 ORIFICE**
This is the hole in line with the axle of the bobbin through which the yarn emerges.

**11 THREADING HOOK**
This is the hook used to pass into the orifice, out of the side hole, catch the yarn or leader and pull it back though the orifice. This action is necessary to start spinning and whenever the yarn breaks. It can be kept to hand by securing it to the wheel on a long cord.

Ashford Traditional single treadle wheel. In production for over 40 years, it is still one of the most popular wheels around.

# Plying and yarn handling tools

THE EQUIPMENT SHOWN HERE WILL ENABLE YOU TO PLY YOUR YARN, MAKE SKEINS, AND WIND BALLS. THE ITEMS HAVE SOME OF THE MOST CHARMING AND QUIRKY NAMES.

A device to support bobbins (normally up to three) enabling the yarn to be drawn off smoothly for plying is called a lazy kate, and is occasionally built into a spinning wheel. The usual tool for winding yarn into skeins of a uniform length is a niddy noddy; weavers' warping boards and skein winders perform the same function and the latter are sometimes available as wheel attachments. The device for supporting a skein while the yarn is wound off is called a swift. Center-pull balls from a ball-winder or nostepinne both look professional and are of practical application. Finally, there are tools to measure the yarn. A yarn gauge is for determining the grist of the yarn—wraps per inch (or per centimeter)—and a McMorran balance gives a reading of yards per pound (or meters per kilo) from a short length of yarn.

## Lazy kate

The bobbins are mounted in different configurations in different designs, but the function is always the same. A tensioning device on a lazy kate is a definite advantage when the yarn is pulled off rapidly during plying—it prevents the bobbin overrunning and avoids yarn tangles.

### Improvised tools

None of these tools are very expensive, but most can also be improvised.

**Lazy kate:** Knitting needles pushed through a shoebox.

**Niddy noddy:** The end of a table or a large book for a sample skein.

**Swift:** A friend's pair of hands.

**Nostepinne:** A small, smooth tube of any sort.

**Yarn gauge:** A standard ruler or notched cardboard.

**McMorran balance:** Accurate domestic weighing scales.

## Niddy noddy

A niddy noddy is a really useful tool, and should be an early priority for beginners. It produces skeins of wholly consistent lengths and can be used to support a singles yarn while twist is set. Petite niddy noddies are available for small sampling quantities.

## Nostepinne

This is a large, handheld wooden dowel, usually slightly tapered, for winding a center-pull ball. It can be a very decorative item when made of attractive wood, or can easily be improvised.

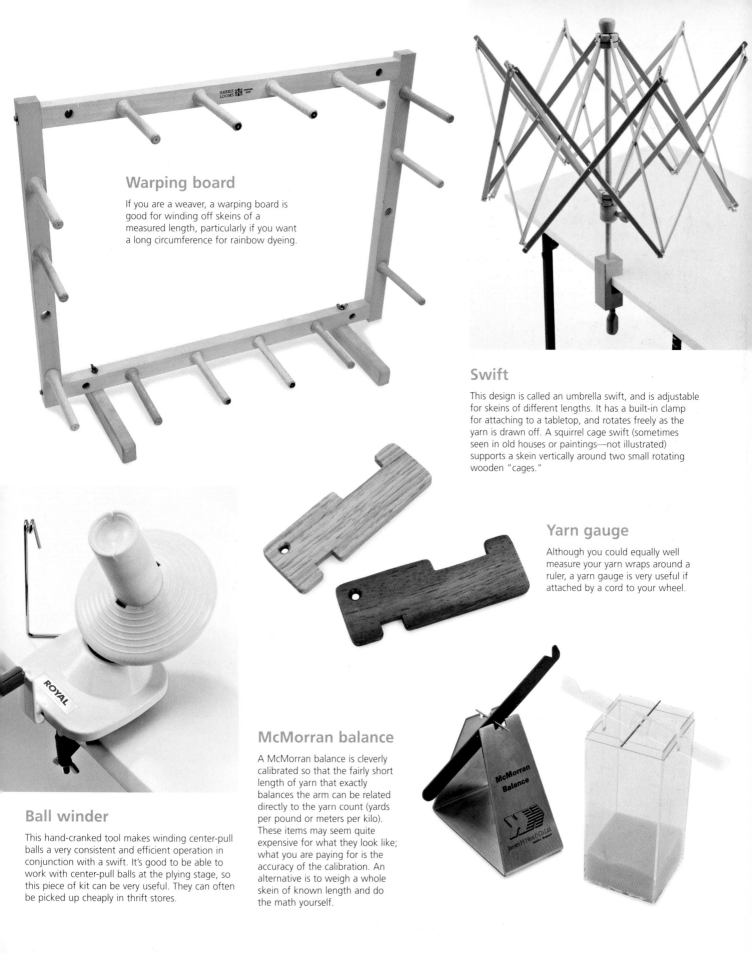

## Warping board

If you are a weaver, a warping board is good for winding off skeins of a measured length, particularly if you want a long circumference for rainbow dyeing.

## Swift

This design is called an umbrella swift, and is adjustable for skeins of different lengths. It has a built-in clamp for attaching to a tabletop, and rotates freely as the yarn is drawn off. A squirrel cage swift (sometimes seen in old houses or paintings—not illustrated) supports a skein vertically around two small rotating wooden "cages."

## Yarn gauge

Although you could equally well measure your yarn wraps around a ruler, a yarn gauge is very useful if attached by a cord to your wheel.

## Ball winder

This hand-cranked tool makes winding center-pull balls a very consistent and efficient operation in conjunction with a swift. It's good to be able to work with center-pull balls at the plying stage, so this piece of kit can be very useful. They can often be picked up cheaply in thrift stores.

## McMorran balance

A McMorran balance is cleverly calibrated so that the fairly short length of yarn that exactly balances the arm can be related directly to the yarn count (yards per pound or meters per kilo). These items may seem quite expensive for what they look like; what you are paying for is the accuracy of the calibration. An alternative is to weigh a whole skein of known length and do the math yourself.

# Fibers

YOUR CHOICE OF FIBER IS ABSOLUTELY FUNDAMENTAL TO PLANNING A YARN, AND THE CHOICE IS EXTREMELY WIDE. MOST PEOPLE START OUT WITH WOOL FROM SHEEP, AND THIS IS A GREAT CHOICE IF YOU HAVE YOUR OWN SHEEP OR CAN SOURCE WOOL LOCALLY. BUT WOOL IS NOT THE DEFAULT FIBER FOR EVERYONE—IN SOME PARTS OF THE WORLD COTTON, SILK, GOAT HAIR, NETTLE, FLAX, AND MANY OTHER FIBERS MIGHT BE THE NATURAL SPINNING CHOICE SIMPLY BECAUSE OF THEIR LOCAL ABUNDANCE.

New fibers are coming onto the market all the time, and some have interesting properties such as antibacterial qualities, good drape, and an affinity for dye. Many are able to lay claim to "green" credentials for their lack of impact on the environment. Whatever the type of fiber, its physical characteristics will always influence the spun yarn.

If you are working toward a particular project, then your choice of fiber type—animal, vegetable, or synthetic—and your choice of specific fiber and its preparation will need to be made carefully with the project in mind.

Whenever you come across a fiber you haven't spun before, try to spin a skein or two in various ways, label them and keep them by for future reference.

## Animal fibers

The fineness, crimp, staple length, and luster of wool all translate directly into the characteristics of the spun yarn, so you should choose your fleece—whether raw fleece or a preparation such as wool top—with that in mind. The fineness of a fiber can be measured in microns or, commonly for wool, as a Bradford count number. With the direct micron measurement, the smaller the number the finer the fiber, but with the Bradford count, it's the other way around. A pretty fine fiber would be around an 80s Bradford count—that's approximately 18–19 microns. A coarse wool—say for making a rug—might be mid-30s Bradford count, or around 40 microns. A fine woolen fiber will also potentially felt fairly readily, so its softness needs to be balanced against the fact that it will be less hardwearing. Coarser fleece may contain "kemp"—rather wiry fibers that contrast with the main fleece quality. It may be possible to remove a couple of kemp fibers as you spin, but a fleece with a lot of kemp may be better avoided.

Animal fibers seen under high magnification show characteristic scales. The friction provided by their scales in conjunction with twist helps make the yarn stable, and it is the embedding of the scales into each other that is stimulated by friction, alkalinity, and thermal shock to make felt.

Silk is almost a category on its own. It may be cultivated or wild, the cultivated variety being reeled from the cocoon of the *Bombyx mori*, fed exclusively on mulberry leaves. In commercial silk production, the silk is literally unwound from the cocoons before the moth emerges and breaks through the fibers. The many and interesting types of silk available to hand spinners, such as mawata and throwster's silk, are waste products from mainstream silk production.

✿ Indicates fibers recommended for beginners to try first.

**JACOB WOOL** ✿
**Comes from:** An ancient breed of horned dual-purpose multicolored sheep.
**Qualities:** Medium staple length, medium softness, natural colors.
**Suitable for:** Knitted outerwear, weaving.

**ALPACA**
**Comes from:** Huacaya and Suri alpacas, members of the llama family, originally native to the South American Andes, now widely reared around the world for their fleece.
**Qualities:** Fine, lustrous, warm, and naturally water repellent.
**Suitable for:** Warm, luxurious garments; can resist wear quite well.

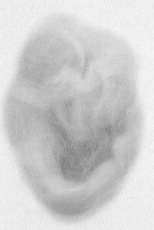

## BLUE-FACED LEICESTER WOOL ✿

**Comes from:** Dual-purpose sheep with characteristic Roman noses and dark blue skin which can be seen through the fleece, hence the name. Blue-faced Leicester is sometimes referred to as BFL wool.

**Qualities:** Medium-long staple length, very soft, mostly white but some natural colors available.

**Suitable for:** Finely spun yarns for soft knitting or weaving.

## WENSLEYDALE WOOL

**Comes from:** One of the largest and heaviest of all sheep breeds, with long ringlet-type locks of fleece.

**Qualities:** Long staple, lustrous, soft but hardwearing.

**Suitable for:** Worsted-spun yarns for robust wear.

## MOHAIR

**Comes from:** The Angora goat, a domestic breed raised for its ringlet-type fleece.

**Qualities:** Soft, lustrous, and very warm.

**Suitable for:** Woolen or worsted spinning; excellent for bouclé yarns.

## CAMEL

**Comes from:** The soft undercoat of the Bactrian (double hump) camel.

**Qualities:** Very fine and soft.

**Suitable for:** Fine spinning for luxury items.

## ANGORA

**Comes from:** The down of the English, French, Satin, and Giant Angora rabbit (as distinct from the Angora goat, which provides mohair).

**Qualities:** Very fine, fluffy, and soft; fairly short staple.

**Suitable for:** Woolen-type spinning for soft garments where a fluffy "halo" is wanted.

## CASHMERE

**Comes from:** The soft downy undercoat of the Cashmere goat, typically combed out (not clipped) during the spring molt and separated from the guard hair.

**Qualities:** Very fine, soft, and warm, natural colors available.

**Suitable for:** Fine, luxurious, warm garments.

## SILK

**Comes from:** The cocoon of the silkworm, principally the mulberry *Bombyx mori*; wild tussah silk comes from more than a dozen silkworm varieties.

**Qualities:** Very fine, soft, strong (less so when wet), and lustrous with a fiber length of 1,000–3,000ft (300–900m) from a cocoon; excellent affinity for dye.

**Suitable for:** A variety of spinning techniques according to the silk preparation, knitting, and weaving.

## HORSEHAIR

**Comes from:** The manes and tails of horses.

**Qualities:** Strong, coarse, and resilient.

**Suitable for:** Specialist woven and craft applications.

## Plant fibers

Fibers are obtained from plants in a range of ways and come from different parts of the plant. What they have in common is that they are normally cellulose-based, and as a consequence, the same sort of synthetic dyes—fiber-reactive cold water dyes, for instance—can be used. Fibers that come from the stem of the plant are called bast fibers, and perhaps most notable in this category is linen from the flax plant. Extracting the fibers is a significant task, and involves rotting away the outside woody covering of the stem using natural enzymes—a process called retting—to reveal the inner fibers for further processing. Several other plants—nettle, hemp and bamboo—can also yield bast fibers.

The other main plant fiber is cotton, widely grown around the world and the fiber commonly used for so much of our clothing and household textiles. Cotton fiber comes from the ripe seedpod of the plant; it has a short staple length and requires less processing than bast fibers. It has simply to be picked, the embedded seeds removed—when carried out mechanically, this process is called "ginning"—and then prepared for the spinning process.

## Synthetic fibers

The manufacture of synthetic fibers for industry is not new, though the early petroleum-based fibers rarely appealed to hand spinners. However, an increasing number of new fibers are being developed that do have hand-spinning appeal, and are being offered in suitably small quantities. These fibers are frequently manufactured from the by-products of other commercial activities and often involve a standard viscose method of production. This means that the cellulose is dissolved in caustic soda and then passed through a spinneret (a device like a fine sieve) into an acid bath, which sets the fiber. The idea may well have come from nature, looking at the natural liquid extrusion spinning process of the silk moth.

Lyocell (created from wood pulp and commonly known by its brand name Tencel®) and bamboo both have excellent drape, and are cellulose-based, so they take fiber-reactive dyes very well. Soy "silk"—another fiber that's popular with hand spinners—is a protein fiber that is a by-product of making tofu.

It can be fun to purchase small quantities of unusual fibers and play around with them (remember to label your samples) before planning a large project.

> ✿ Indicates fibers recommended for beginners to try first.

## Plant fibers

**COTTON**
**Comes from:** The fibers in the seed boll of the genus *Gossypium*, of which *G. hirsutum* represents most of the world's production.
**Qualities:** Short-staple, cool, and breathable fine fiber.
**Suitable for:** Woolen-type spinning yarns for weaving and knitting.

## Synthetic fibers

**1 BAMBOO ✿**
**Comes from:** Bamboo viscose, mainly grown in China and normally to organic growing and production standards.
**Qualities:** Antibacterial, absorbent, and breathable; hypo-allergenic; soft; good sheen and drape.
**Suitable for:** Worsted-type spinning, blending with other fibers, knitting, weaving.

**LINEN**
**Comes from:** The central stem of the flax plant, *Linum usitatissimum*.
**Qualities:** Strong (especially when wet), smooth, low elasticity, creases easily.
**Suitable for:** Worsted-type spinning yarns, mainly for weaving.

**RAMIE** ✿
**Comes from:** The cortex of China Grass, a flowering plant in the nettle family *Urticacea*.
**Qualities:** Crisp, strong (stronger wet than dry), lustrous, low elasticity, poorer dye affinity than cotton.
**Suitable for:** Worsted-type spinning yarns, mainly for weaving.

**JUTE**
**Comes from:** The stem and outer skin of plants in the genus *Corchorus*, the fiber being extracted by retting.
**Qualities:** Long, strong, and coarse.
**Suitable for:** Strong cordage for woven mats and basketwork.

**ABACA**
**Comes from:** The leaves of the abaca (*Musa textilis*), a relative of the banana and indigenous to the Philippines.
**Qualities:** Strong and hardwearing, cheap, resistant to salt water.
**Suitable for:** Rope, cordage for woven mats and basketwork.

**TENCEL®**
**Comes from:** Bleached wood pulp; manufactured by a viscose process.
**Qualities:** Soft, good sheen and drape, wrinkle resistant, strong.
**Suitable for:** Worsted-type spinning, blending with other fibers, knitting, weaving.

**SOY FIBER**
**Comes from:** The soybean residue left over from the manufacture of tofu.
**Qualities:** Good sheen and drape, as moisture absorbent as cotton but with better ventilation properties.
**Suitable for:** Worsted-type spinning, blending with other fibers, knitting, weaving.

**INGEO**
**Comes from:** The polylactic acid present in corn, made in a manufacturing process free of petrochemicals.
**Qualities:** Good moisture absorption and ventilation properties, drape, softness, and warmth; biodegradable.
**Suitable for:** Worsted-type spinning, blending with other fibers, knitting, weaving.

**MILK PROTEIN**
**Comes from:** The proteins present in milk, manufactured in a similar process to soy fiber.
**Qualities:** Soft, good sheen and drape, absorbent.
**Suitable for:** Worsted-type spinning, blending with other fibers, knitting, weaving.

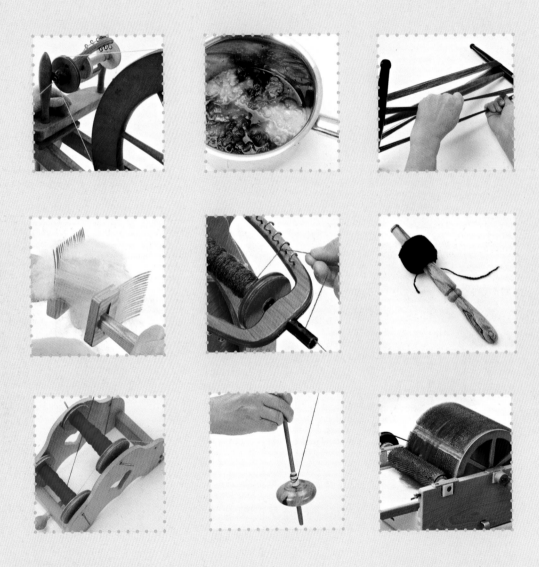

*Chapter 2*

# Techniques

*This chapter takes you through the entire spinning process, from preparing fiber, dyeing before or after spinning, and using a spindle or wheel, through to plying, making skeins, and finishing the yarn. Step-by-step photography shows all the techniques in clear detail. Panels give tips for beginners and further ideas for more advanced experimentation.*

# Scouring

FIBERS IN THEIR RAW STATE CONTAIN DIRT AND GREASE, WHICH IS REMOVED BY THE  PROCESS KNOWN AS SCOURING. ALTHOUGH IT IS POSSIBLE TO SPIN "IN THE GREASE," SCOURING IS SOMETIMES ESSENTIAL, SUCH AS WHEN YOU WANT TO DYE FIBER BEFORE SPINNING.

Scouring differs from ordinary washing in the choice of cleaning agent and the way the fiber is handled. Most fibers must be handled carefully, avoiding agitation, thermal shock (rapid change of water temperature), and harsh detergents, otherwise woolen fibers may become felted. A loose mass of fibers can easily drift apart and end up either matted or blocking your drains by leaving too much fiber in the rinsing water. For fine fleece, use a conventional domestic mesh laundry bag, or, for other very fine fibers, you could improvise a fine washing bag from old pantyhose (tights). A salad spinner is great as a small-scale spin dryer. Never attempt to tumble dry loose fiber—always finish by drying naturally.

## Dirt extraction

A surprising amount of dirt is extracted from even a very small amount of raw fleece. Watch out for fleece assumed to be beige that is actually snow-white when washed.

## Scouring raw fleece

Here, a small amount of raw Jacob fleece is being scoured. As it holds together quite well, it wasn't necessary to use a net bag in this case.

**1** Prepare a bowl of hot water with a generous squirt of dishwashing liquid or special scouring detergent, and place the fibers on top. Allow them to sink naturally without pressing down to avoid air pockets and to achieve better saturation.

**3** Remove excess water by whirling the fiber in an old salad spinner.

**2** Gently move the fibers in the water and leave to soak. Lift the fiber mass gently and allow to drain. Prepare a rinsing bath at a very similar temperature and repeat the process described in Step 1, allowing the fiber to sink into the water until the rinse water is clean.

**4** The clean fibers, having dried naturally, emerge from the process neither felted nor tangled and are ready to be prepared for spinning.

# Teasing

A LOCK OF ANIMAL FIBER OR A PREPARED TOP CAN BE TOO DENSE FOR SPINNING DIRECTLY. TEASING IS THE PROCESS OF SPREADING OUT THE FIBERS INTO A THINNER, BUT WIDER, MASS, SEPARATING OUT TANGLES AND FREEING TRAPPED VEGETATION OR FOREIGN MATTER.

If you want to spin natural fleece with the minimum of preparation, gently teasing the fleece lock by lock will give you a perfectly acceptable starting point from which you can spin directly in either worsted or woolen methods (see pages 54–57).

## Teasing a lock

Teasing locks into a more open formation greatly helps the carding process.

**1** This is a lock of raw, fine fleece that can be prepared for spinning direct using only the hands. Raw locks are compact and dirty. Note the dirtier end against the inner clean white fleece.

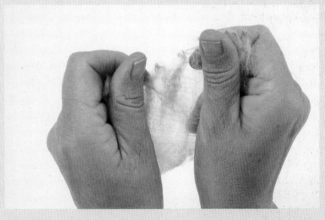

**3** Hold the sides of a lock between two hands and gently pull apart, holding the fiber between the flank of the thumbs and the fingers.

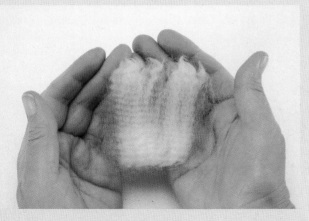

**2** Tease just one lock at a time for even results.

**4** The lock is now fully opened up, and in many cases, it can be spun directly without further preparation.

# Carding

CARDING MORE THOROUGHLY OPENS UP THE
FIBERS AND FREES THEM OF TANGLES AND DEBRIS
THAN TEASING ALONE.

Carding may also be used as a blending process for
different fibers or colors (see pages 34–35), and the end
preparation will tend to contain some variety of fiber
length (consequently, a different preparation is used for
worsted spinning). Carding may be done using a pair of
hand carders or using a drum carding machine.

## Hand carding

Carding by hand involves removing tangles from
the fiber and creating an evenly prepared sheet of
fiber known as a batt.

**1** Rest the carder
flat on your lap
with the teeth
facing upward
and the handle
facing toward
your left side.
Notice that the
teeth are hooked.
Lay a small
amount of fiber
across the carder,
pulling gently
against the teeth.
Do not overload
the carder.

**2** With the filled carder still resting on your lap, grip
the handle of the filled carder and hold the empty
carder, teeth downward, in your right hand.

**3** Begin stroking the right carder gently across the
left, starting at the free edge where the fiber
protrudes and gradually working across. You are
aiming to enable the fiber to be brushed out
smoothly without embedding the two sets of teeth
together. After several strokes, a lot of the fiber
will have transferred to the right carder.

**4** Transfer the fiber
on the right carder
onto the left carder.
Turn the right carder
so that the handle is
upward and the
teeth face left. Hook
the fiber onto the
left carder starting
at the handle edge
and, with a
sweeping action,
release the fiber onto
the right. Repeat
Steps 3–4.

**5** Now transfer any
fiber remaining on the
left carder to the right
carder in a similar way
and repeat Steps 3 and
4 again. Continue to
repeat these steps until
the fiber is sufficiently
uniform for your
purpose, and pick out
any reluctant tangles
and foreign matter by
hand as you do so.
Finish with all of the
fiber transferred back
onto the left carder.

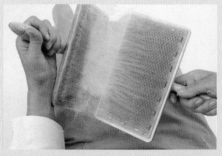

**6** Flip over the right carder and use its tines to lift
the carded layer of fiber (known as a batt) free.
Turn the left carder over and lay the batt flat onto
the back ready to make a rolag (see pages 36–37)
for woolen spinning (see pages 56–57).

# Drum carding

A drum carder is a useful piece of equipment when you have a large amount of fiber for processing and, as a larger item, it is something often bought by a group or spinners' guild for shared use. It consists of two drums—large and small—and a handle for turning the drums at different speeds, as well as a feed tray.

**3** Take hold of the forward portion of the sheet of fibers (the batt) and slowly start to rotate the handle in reverse, maintaining a little tension on the batt, and release it fully from the drum. This is known as "doffing the batt." Inspect the batt for thoroughness of carding; it may need more. If so, split the batt lengthwise into two or more strips and tease each out to the approximate width of the smaller drum and repeat the process. As with hand carding, the carded batt is now ready to make a rolag for woolen spinning.

**1** Start by placing a small amount of fiber (such as teased fleece [see page 31]) on the feed tray with the tips just reaching the small drum and start to turn the handle. The fiber will attach itself to the smaller drum and will transfer to the larger one. Do not hang onto the fiber on the feed tray, otherwise it will embed itself too deeply on the smaller drum, prevent effective carding, and make for a more difficult cleaning job later. Continue to place more fiber on the feed tray until all the fiber has been processed or the larger drum is full and the teeth are covered.

**2** Stop the larger drum when the channel in the card clothing is at the top. Run the supplied metal rod along the channel, and lift upward to break the layers of fiber apart in preparation for removing them.

## Expert advice

### Removing the batt

It can be helpful to place a dishcloth over the larger drum and roll the batt around that rather than simply lifting it off. This can help a delicate batt of fine fibers hold together better.

# Blending

THERE ARE MANY TIMES YOU WILL WANT TO SPIN YARNS CONTAINING MORE THAN ONE FIBER, USUALLY IN ORDER TO BENEFIT FROM THE DIFFERENT CHARACTERISTICS OF THE FIBERS USED.

If you have a slippery fiber such as dog or cat fur, a 50/50 mix with soft wool helps anchor the more slippery fiber in the finished yarn, and makes the spinning process easier. The lustrous qualities of silk will be apparent in a yarn made from a blend with only a minor proportion of silk—perhaps as little as 10 percent.

A fiber blend normally needs to be based on fibers with similar staple lengths so that both fibers draw out similarly during the spinning process. Prepare each fiber individually first if starting with raw fiber—for example if your blend contains wool and the finished blend is to be carded, card the wool on its own first.

To blend two fibers on hand cards, sandwich the more slippery fiber between two layers of the other, or the one forming the minor proportion of the blend. Card as normal (see page 32) to create a blended batt. The more times you transfer the fibers between the two cards, the more thorough will be the finished blend. More thorough is not always best—a very slight blend can give interesting results. But whether a thoroughly mixed blend is your aim or not, be consistent about the proportions used in each blend for a large project. You can achieve this by weighing out batches of each fiber—enough for, say, no more than about ten cards' worth—which you can then allocate into ten piles for blending. Fibers of the same length can also be blended by combing (see page 40).

## Color blending

You can achieve lovely effects by blending different colors of fiber on either hand cards or a drum carder. The placement of the colors in the starting position on hand cards determines how the finished blend will look. For a fairly even color blend, you can simply sandwich a layer of one color between two thin layers of the other, just as with blending different fiber types. To create a shaded batt or rolag, place a different color in the central zone of the card.

**2** As the active card is flipped through 180 degrees when transferring fiber between the cards, the colors on the outside edges automatically mix with each other.

**1** The colors are placed side by side on the left carder to show how the carding process mixes the colors on opposite sides.

**3** Continuing to card as normal, the colors become quite uniformly blended.

**4** The completed blend made into a rolag ready for spinning (see pages 36–37).

## Blending fibers

A blend of two or more fiber types will show the characteristics of each in the result. A small amount of a luxury fiber can influence the yarn in a beneficial way. Where possible, aim to choose fibers with a similar staple length and have each fiber already carded individually if starting from fleece.

**1** Lay a thin layer of the fiber with more grip (here, the brown fiber) on the card followed by a thin layer of the more slippery fiber (beige).

**2** Lock the slippery layer in place by adding a further very fine layer of the first fiber on top.

**3** Card as usual until the two fibers are sufficiently blended. Avoid the temptation to over-blend or you may create noils (see Glossary, page 141).

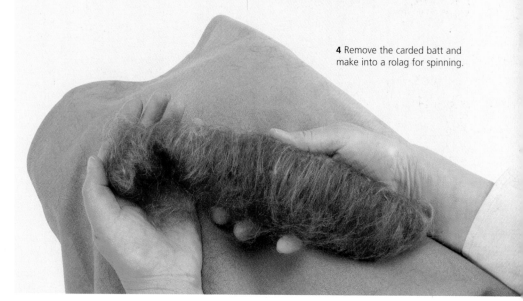

**4** Remove the carded batt and make into a rolag for spinning.

## >> Try this next

If you are dealing with two fibers of very dissimilar staple length, you will find it easier to blend them if you cut the longer one with sharp scissors into a similar length to that of the shorter fiber.

The long staple of the white Wensleydale wool would be difficult to process on hand cards and would not blend well at its full length with the yellow Merino.

Open out the Wensleydale slightly on the hand cards and cut the staple in half. The cut down fiber can then be blended easily with the Merino in the usual way.

# Making rolags and punis

ROLAGS AND PUNIS ARE ROLLED ARRANGEMENTS OF FIBERS, RATHER LIKE A JELLY ROLL OR SWISS ROLL.

The fiber supply for spinning is drawn from the end of the roll and this is the preparation for woolen spinning. Rolls made from wool and similar fibers are normally called "rolags." Smaller, tighter rolls made from short-stapled fiber such as cotton or throwster's silk are normally called "punis."

## Making a rolag from a hand-carded batt

Starting with the result of your hand carding, the batt, the next step is to make it into a rolag. This is the standard method.

**1** Place the batt on the smooth back of one of the hand cards in your lap with the handle of the carder facing away from you. Beginning at the fiber edge nearest to you, lift up the loose fringe of fibers and fold over.

**2** Gently roll up the fibers into a fairly loose arrangement, and use the back of the other carder to roll the rolag gently backward and forward. It should be very light when completed and not too compacted, otherwise drawing out the fiber could be a problem.

## Alternative method direct from hand carders

Rather than making a rolag from a batt removed from hand carders, you may prefer to make the rolag directly from the batt still on the carder.

**1** When carding is complete, start to roll directly from the carder, using the right carder to "nudge" the fibers into a roll.

**2** Finish by gently rolling across the face of the left carder using very light pressure. Because you are working with the direction of the carder teeth (rather than against them when you are carding), the fibers are released rather than being gripped.

# Making a puni

A carded batt of short fiber made into a compact mini rolag is known as a puni. Use carders with fine teeth if possible and have a smooth dowel rod on hand.

**1** Lay a perfectly smooth dowel rod across the batt and roll the batt around the rod. Still on the dowel rod, smooth any loose ends either by rolling the stick on the smooth back of a carder or by cupping your fingers around it and twirling the stick. This is done so that short-stapled fibers such as cotton are adequately secured.

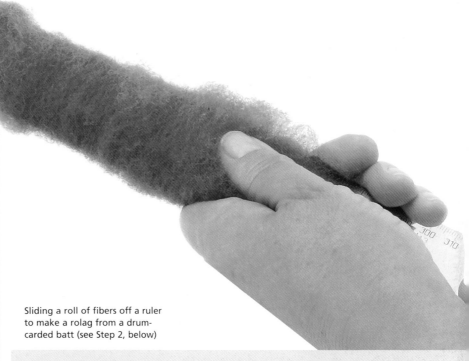

Sliding a roll of fibers off a ruler to make a rolag from a drum-carded batt (see Step 2, below)

**2** Slide the puni off the stick and spin from the end as for a rolag.

# Making a rolag from a drum-carded batt

The batt from a drum carder is very much bigger than that from hand carders—it is too much fiber for effective spinning. It needs to be made into a number of rolags using a different approach.

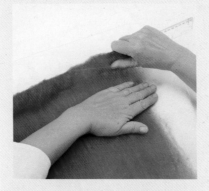

**1** Lay the batt of fibers flat on a cloth—a dishcloth for example. Lay a ruler across the batt near the end, across the fiber direction, not parallel to it.

**2** Fold the loose fringe of fibers over the ruler and then roll the ruler over twice. Press your forearm across the fiber batt just above the ruler to hold the fibers securely, and pull the ruler away from the batt to separate the fibers. Slide the roll of fibers off the ruler, and you will have a rolag that is long (the full width of the drum), but contains an appropriate amount of fiber for spinning. Repeat the process until the remaining batt is used up.

**3** The fiber can now be removed from the face of the carder as a rolag rather than as a batt.

# Pre-drafting

THE PRE-DRAFTING TECHNIQUE EFFECTIVELY SEPARATES THE WORSTED SPINNING PROCESS INTO TWO PARTS: DRAFTING THE FIBER TO THE THICKNESS YOU WANT AND ADDING THE AMOUNT OF TWIST YOU WANT. IT IS RARELY ESSENTIAL BUT CAN BE USEFUL IN A VARIETY OF CIRCUMSTANCES.

The different methods of pre-drafting—pre-drafting the full thickness or splitting into "fingers" first—give similar results when working with a solid color, but results that are visually quite different when working with variegated colors.

## Notes for beginners

When you are just starting out, you will have a lot on your plate trying to coordinate all aspects of the spinning process at the same time. If you pre-draft your fiber to the actual thickness you want, you have only the twisting process to concentrate on, and you should find you can achieve a consistent yarn more easily.

## Pre-drafting a commercial top

Many exciting fibers, including colors and blends, are available prepared commercially in a "top." This dense fiber supply benefits from being opened up (or pre-drafted) before spinning.

**2** Gripping firmly, give a sharp tug until you feel the fiber supply give slightly. Move both hands along the top, keeping them the same distance apart and repeat along the length of the fiber supply you are preparing.

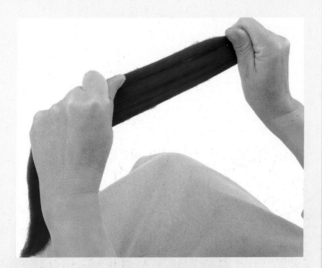

**1** Beginning at one end of the top, hold a section between your hands, which must be a distance apart just a little more than the staple length of the fiber.

## Splitting a top into "fingers"

This method is useful for rainbow-dyed tops where you want the color changes to repeat quite frequently in the spun yarn.

**1** Part a section of the top at the end and pull apart, splitting the top lengthwise into two.

**2** Repeat the splitting process until you have the number of "fingers" of equal thickness you want. Notice that splitting the top in this way gives fibers a tendency to fly away where the top was torn apart.

**3** Now pre-draft each finger as described in Steps 2–4 of "Pre-drafting a commercial top" (below), and the fly-away fibers will reunite with the main fiber supply to give a smoother spinning preparation. For a rainbow top, the thickness of each finger, as well as the length of the color section, will determine the amount of a particular color of fiber to be spun before a color change occurs.

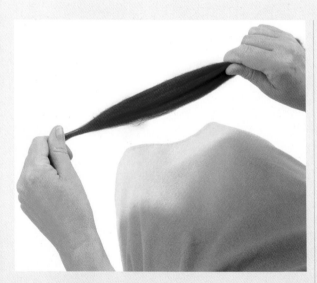

**3** Starting at one end again, and with your hands in the same position, pull your hands gently apart and work along the length of the top.

**4** Repeat Step 3 as many times as necessary, drafting a little thinner each time until you have a sliver of the final thickness you want.

**5** Temporarily store the drafted fiber so that it won't tangle as you spin. For wheel spinning, make a figure-eight around your fingers, which rest in your lap. For spindle spinning, try wrapping the drafted fiber around your wrist.

### Expert advice

#### Spinning thick yarns

When you want a thick singles yarn, treadling the wheel or twirling the spindle may add twist more quickly than you can cope with it, and your yarn can easily become over-twisted. You can overcome this difficulty by pre-drafting the fiber to the appropriate thickness first, enabling you to store lengths of spun yarn at a rapid rate without having to draft quickly and consistently.

## Using a dog comb

The simple dog comb can transform a teased lock of fleece into an excellent starting point for worsted spinning.

**1** Have a protective sturdy cloth or piece of leather on your lap, and firmly grip a lock of wool by the cut end. Tap the teeth of the comb through the wool onto your lap. Although the tool is a comb, it is not at all like combing your hair because you do not draw the teeth along the length of the fibers.

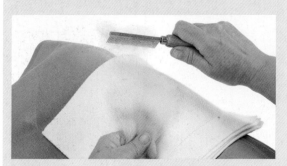

**2** When the tips are nicely opened up, turn the lock around and repeat the tapping process on the other end.

**4** Pre-draft the long fibers slightly into a delicate roving (see pages 38–39).

# Combing

THE MAIN DIFFERENCE BETWEEN THE CARDING AND COMBING PROCESSES IS THAT COMBING REMOVES SHORT FIBERS AS WELL AS THOROUGHLY OPENING UP EACH FIBER AND FREEING IT OF TANGLES AND DEBRIS.

Combing is the preparation necessary for pure worsted spinning (see pages 54–55). Like carding, combing may also be used as a blending process for different fibers or colors. Combing may be done using a simple dog comb, a pair of mini hand combs, or a set of English wool combs.

The purpose of combing is to produce a smooth, parallel preparation of fiber of consistent length, the shorter fibers being removed in the process; it is the absence of short fibers that is one of the defining characteristics of worsted spinning. The progression from dog comb to mini combs to English wool combs represents increasing cost of the equipment, and reducing portability, offset by increasing productivity: mini combs and English wool combs can handle larger quantities of fiber and make it easier to draw out a good roving than a dog comb.

**3** Now that the lock is opened up fully, you can use the comb like a hair comb to remove the short fibers, leaving only the long ones behind.

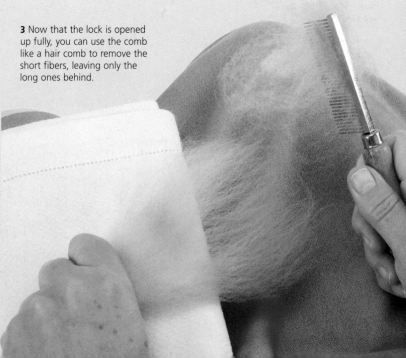

## English wool combs

A set of English wool combs is a fearsome piece of kit! The combs are heavy and the tines sharp. Take great care that you do not drop one or leave them unattended where they could cause an accident, particularly when children are around. The more specialized process of using these combs is not illustrated here.

Passing the mini combs through the fleece (see Step 2, right)

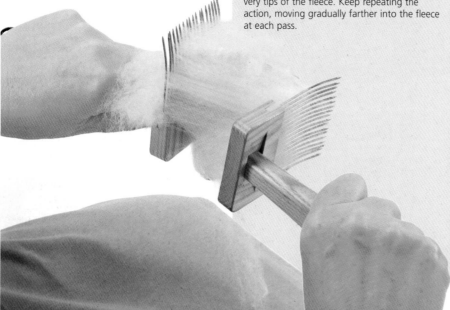

## Using mini hand combs

Mini combs, though small and lightweight, can transform a quantity of teased locks into a uniform roving for worsted spinning.

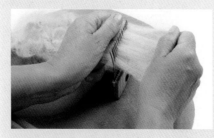

**1** Mount a small quantity of teased locks onto the tines of one comb; the base of the locks should extend about ½in (1cm) on the handle side and the tips should lie loose on the other side. Hold the filled comb in your left hand, tines uppermost.

**3** When there are no more good fibers left on the left-hand comb, remove the remainder and discard. Change hands and repeat the process until you have a uniform arrangement of fibers on the comb.

**2** Take the other comb in your right hand with the tines facing away from you and, with a sweeping motion, pass the comb through the very tips of the fleece. Keep repeating the action, moving gradually farther into the fleece at each pass.

**4** With your hand, stroke the fibers into the shape of an artist's brush. Holding the loaded comb firmly in your lap, pull on the tip of the "brush" and begin to draw off a roving of fiber. Reposition your grip on the fiber supply frequently so that a continuous roving can be drawn off.

**5** Several rovings can be laid on top of each other and the combined fiber arrangement drafted a little more for a consistent fiber preparation for worsted spinning. A roving can be given a slight twist and coiled for storage.

# Dyeing

THIS BOOK IS NOT A DETAILED DYE MANUAL—THERE ARE MANY GOOD BOOKS DEVOTED TO THE SUBJECT— BUT AIMS TO GIVE YOU A SIMPLE OVERVIEW OF THE DYEING PROCESS FROM A SPINNER'S PERSPECTIVE.

There are many different dyeing techniques—natural dyeing, tie-dyeing, dip-dyeing, to name just a few. Here, we cover two important dyeing methods: even one-color dyeing (also known as level dyeing or solid dyeing) and rainbow dyeing.

## Fiber-reactive dyes vs. acid dyes

Protein fibers (such as wool) and cellulose fibers (such as cotton) react to different types of dye, so it is essential to match the fiber and dye types correctly. Acid dyes are for protein fibers; the dye process requires heat and the dyes are easy to store in solution without losing their potency. Fiber-reactive dyes are for cellulose; the dye process uses cold water but they quickly lose their potency in solution as the dye molecules bond with the water as well as with fiber.

## One-color dyeing

Dyeing all of your batch of fiber or yarn one even shade is known as one-color dyeing. Even though you can opt to dye your yarn after spinning, there are advantages to dyeing the fiber beforehand. Color variations will not show after you prepare the fiber for spinning, as you can blend light and dark fibers.

## One-color dyeing with acid dyes

The stock solutions that you make here will make measuring the small quantities required in craft dyeing easy, and the solutions will keep well without losing their effectiveness.

**You will need:**
• 1 level tsp (5g) acid dye powder plus 1pt (500ml) water
• 1½oz (50g) sodium sulfate (Glauber's salt) plus 1pt (500ml) water
• Household vinegar (see method for quantity)
• Non-reactive stove-top stainless steel dyepot
• Thermometer (optional)

**General preparation:**
**1** Observing all the standard safety precautions (see page 140), make up 1 percent dye standard stock solutions from individual colors of dye. Make a paste by adding a few drops of water to the powder, and stirring, then adding about half the total quantity of water you need as boiling water and stir until dissolved. Top up with cold water to make up the exact total quantity of 1pt (or 500ml).
**2** In a similar way, make up a 10 percent stock solution of sodium sulfate. This is your leveling agent.
**3** Have ready some standard household vinegar—distilled white vinegar is ideal. This is your acid.

## One-color dyeing with fiber reactive dyes

Fiber-reactive dyes in solution soon lose their intensity. Avoid making up much more dye solution than you will use within a few days.

**You will need:**
• 1 level tsp (5g) acid dye powder plus 1pt (500ml) water—or smaller quantities keeping the same proportions
• 1½oz (50g) soda ash crystals (sodium carbonate) plus 1pt (500ml) water
• 3½oz (100g) common household or table salt (sodium chloride) plus 1pt (500ml) water
• Non-reactive dyepot (such as a glass jar)

**General preparation**
**1** Observing all the standard safety precautions (see page 131), mix the measured dye powder with a few drops of water to form a paste. Add ½pt (250ml) boiling water and stir well. Add ½pt (250ml) of cold water.
**2** In a similar way, make up a 10 percent stock solution of soda ash and a 20 percent stock solution of salt.

## Fiber-reactive dye: ingredients based on depth of shade

| DEPTH OF SHADE (VOLUME OF DYE SOLUTION TO DRY WEIGHT OF FIBER) | VOLUME OF 10% STOCK SODA SOLUTION TO DRY WEIGHT OF FIBER | VOLUME OF 20% STOCK SALT SOLUTION TO DRY WEIGHT OF FIBER |
|---|---|---|
| 1% (1fl oz per 1oz weight or 1ml per 1g) | 0.5% (½fl oz per 1oz weight or 0.5ml per 1g) | 5% (5fl oz per 1oz weight or 5ml per 1g) |
| 2% (2fl oz per 1oz weight or 2ml per 1g) | 1% (1fl oz per 1oz weight or 1ml per 1g) | 6% (6fl oz per 1oz weight or 6ml per 1g) |
| 3% (3fl oz per 1oz weight or 3ml per 1g) | 1.25% (1¼fl oz per 1oz weight or 1.25ml per 1g) | 7% (7fl oz per 1oz weight or 7ml per 1g) |

**Method:**

**1** Pour cold or tepid water into the dyepot—roughly 30:1, i.e. 30fl oz per 1oz weight of dry fiber (or 30ml per 1g). Add 1fl oz per 1oz weight of dry fiber (or 1ml per 1g) of both sodium sulfate solution and vinegar and stir well. Add the wetted out fiber to the pan and start to heat very gently. Temporarily remove the fiber before the pan gets above blood heat and add the appropriate total quantity of dye stock. You will need about 3 percent of your fiber weight for a fairly saturated color, about 1 percent for a pale color. This is

known as the depth of shade (DOS). You will probably wish to blend stock colors for subtle results, so your 3 percent or other DOS is the total quantity of stock solutions altogether.

**2** Stir the dye solution well and return the fiber to the dyepot, continuing to raise the heat slowly to boiling point. For silk, do not heat above simmering point, otherwise the sheen may be damaged. Hold at this temperature until the dyepot is exhausted (only clear liquid remaining) or for about 20 minutes.

**3** Let cool, then rinse out in water of the same temperature, blot on an old towel, and let dry naturally. Avoid over-handling wet protein fiber and exposing it to temperature shocks, otherwise you may cause felting to begin.

**Method:**

**1** First decide on the depth of shade you wish to use: this dictates the quantities of the other solutions you need. 3 percent is fairly saturated, 1 percent quite pale. Use the table on the left and note down the quantity of each liquid required reading across the relevant row. Figure the volume of water required in addition to bring the total

liquid volume up to 30:1—30fl oz per 1oz weight of dry fiber (or 30ml per 1g). Pour all the liquids (dye solution, soda, salt and extra water) into the dye vessel and stir well. Add the fiber.

**2** Move or gently stir the fiber in the dyepot to expose fiber to dye evenly; do so constantly for the first five minutes. Leave the fibers in the

dyepot for about two hours in total, gently stirring at intervals of about 15 minutes.

**3** Remove the fibers from the dyepot and rinse in warm running water until the water runs clear. When fully rinsed, wash in a soapy solution, rinse again, blot on an old towel, and let dry naturally.

# Rainbow dyeing

Rainbow dyeing, in contrast to one-color dyeing, means using several different colors at the same time with the intention of keeping plenty of color differentiation. The colors will naturally blend where the dyestuffs bleed together in the fiber package, giving pleasingly random results.

With rainbow dyeing, your aim is to limit the ability of the dyestuff to run easily throughout the whole package of fiber. This means using a very limited amount of water, omitting specific leveling agents like sodium sulfate, and packing the fiber closely together. The dye stock solutions are poured (undiluted for strong shades) directly onto distinct areas of the wetted fibers, making sure they have fully penetrated, then the dye process is completed as usual. When using acid dyes on a fiber top, a useful method is to wrap the dye-soaked top in plastic wrap. You can then heat the package by steaming or microwaving. For washed fleece, you can closely pack locks upright into a dyepot and use a low level of water to good effect.

## Notes for beginners

• Generally, protein and cellulose fibers require different types of dye in order to make a successful chemical bond and a good, lasting color. Protein fibers include wool, and other animal-hair fibers such as mohair, alpaca, cashmere, and silk. Cellulose fibers include cotton, flax (linen), ramie, bamboo, and so on.

• Of the main classes of synthetic dyes, I suggest you try acid dyes for protein fibers and cold water fiber-reactive dyes for cellulose. Silk is in a slightly unusual position in that it takes both acid and fiber-reactive dyes readily.

• Various natural dyes such as plant extracts can also be used to good effect, normally requiring a mordant—a chemical assistant to the dyeing process that enables the dye to bond successfully with the fiber.

## Rainbow dyeing with acid dyes

The stock solutions that you need here are the same ones you need for acid one-color dyeing—there is no need to make up separate solutions if you already have some to hand. It is safer to work with solutions rather than powders and the results are a little more controllable.

**You will need:**
• For each color, 1 level tsp (5g) acid dye powder plus 1pt (500ml) water
• Household vinegar (see method for quantity)
• Non-reactive stove-top dyepot, preferably stainless steel
• Plastic measuring syringe
• Thermometer (optional)

**General preparation:**
1 Observing all the standard safety precautions (see page 140), mix the measured dye powder with a few drops of water to form a paste. Add half the total quantity of water as boiling water, stir well and add the remaining half of the water cold.
2 Have ready some standard household vinegar—distilled white vinegar is ideal. This is your acid.

## Rainbow dyeing with fiber-reactive dyes

Stock solutions are the same for fiber-reactive one-color dyeing—there is no need to make up separate solutions. It is safer to work with solutions rather than powders.

**You will need:**
• For each color, small quantities of stock dye solution in proportion to 1 level tsp (5g) fiber-reactive dye powder per 1pt (500ml) water
• 1½oz (50g) soda ash crystals (sodium carbonate) plus 1pt (500ml) water
• 3½oz (100g) common household or table salt (sodium chloride) plus 1pt (500ml) water
• Roll of plastic wrap
• Plastic measuring syringe

**General preparation**
1 Observing all the standard safety precautions (see page 140), mix the measured dye powder with a few drops of water to form a paste. Add ½pt (250ml) boiling water and stir well. Add ½pt (250ml) of cold water.
2 In a similar way, make up a 10 percent stock solution of soda ash and a 20 percent stock solution of salt.

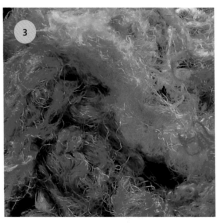

**Method:**

**1** Prepare the dyepot by adding 1fl oz per 1oz weight of dry fiber (or 1ml per 1g) of vinegar to a minimal amount of water and stir well. Add the closely packed fibers, packing locks upright. Add different dye solutions to distinct areas using a plastic syringe, aiming for local penetration without too much general mixing. You do not have to be precise about the amount of dyestuff for rainbow dyeing, but once you use more than about 3 percent of dye in total, the fiber may be unable to take up all of the dye.

**2** Bring slowly to simmering point without stirring or agitating the pan to avoid too much mixing of the colors before the dye fixes on the fiber. Continue to simmer for about 20 minutes or until the dyes are absorbed and the water in the pan is clear. With a low level of water, take care not to let the pan boil dry.

**3** Allow to cool, rinse and wash gently, and allow to dry as normal. Further color blending can be achieved at the carding or combing stage.

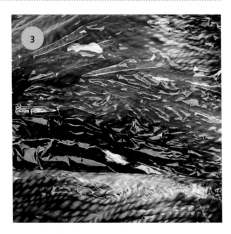

**Method:**

**1** Lay out a sheet of plastic wrap and a skein of cellulose yarn (cotton yarn in this case) on a work surface. Working to 3 percent depth of shade overall, measure out 3fl oz of dye solution per 1oz dry weight of fiber (or 3ml per 1g of dry fiber). For each 3 units of dye, add 1¼ units of soda solution and 7 units of salt solution. Apply the liquid directly to the yarn using a syringe.

**2** Press the dye into the yarn to ensure proper penetration, adding additional colors. Adjacent colors will blend to an extent automatically, but you can emphasize this by overlapping color applications.

**3** Cover the wet yarn with plastic wrap and roll into a tube. Leave for several hours or overnight for the dyes to set. Rinse, wash, and dry in the usual way.

# Spindle spinning

ONE OF THE SIMPLEST WAYS OF MAKING A QUANTITY OF YARN IS TO USE A HAND SPINDLE. PER HOUR OF SPINNING IT MAY BE A SLOWER PROCESS THAN USING A WHEEL, BUT THE PORTABILITY OF A SPINDLE MEANS YOU CAN SPIN IN SPARE MOMENTS AND THIS MAY INCREASE YOUR PRODUCTIVITY.

The spindle provides the means of adding the essential twist into the fiber, keeping it under light tension while doing so, and storing the spun yarn. The techniques of woolen or worsted spinning apply equally to spinning using either a simple spindle or a spinning wheel. See pages 16–17 for details of different types of spindles available. To start, you will need a small supply of prepared fiber, and a spindle with a leader yarn attached. I recommend you use a doubled leader with a loop in the end. In the following sequences, green arrows show spinning direction and red arrows show hand direction.

### Notes for beginners

As your spinning progresses, a suspended spindle gets appreciably heavier, which means increased tension on your spinning. So you may need to stop before your spindle is absolutely full otherwise the yarn will start to break regularly.

## Spinning with a bottom-whorl suspended spindle

The principle of spinning with a suspended spindle is to set it in motion to add twist, allow its weight to provide the necessary tension to keep the newly spun yarn under control, and to use its shaft to store the yarn.

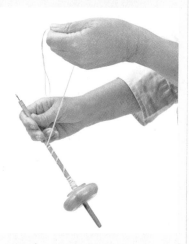

**1** Twirl the top of the shaft clockwise while holding the leader at an angle of about 90 degrees, spiraling the leader up the shaft toward the top.

**2** Secure the leader to the top of the spindle with a half hitch (if it has a notch) or by wrapping around the hook if it has one. Leave about 6in (15cm) of the leader yarn free.

**3** Draw out a few fibers, pass them through the loop in the leader, double the end over, and pinch between forefinger and thumb of the left hand.

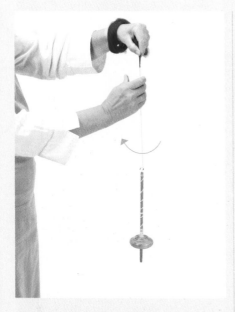

**4** Wrap the unspun fiber loosely round the wrist to keep it out of the way as you spin. Still holding the join together with the left hand, use the right hand to start the spindle rotating clockwise for a Z-twist yarn.

**6** Repeat Step 5 as long as the spindle is still turning and hasn't yet reached the floor.

**8** When the spindle is about to touch the floor, keep the newly spun yarn under some tension while you undo the half hitch or unwrap from the hook.

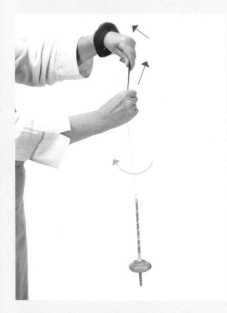

**5** Now use the right hand to hold the join and draft more fibers by gently pulling back with the left hand. Slide the right hand along the drafted fibers; the twist will follow behind your fingers to create spun yarn.

**7** As the spindle slows to a stop (keep an eye on it or it will start to turn backward and untwist your spun yarn), give it another flick to maintain clockwise rotation.

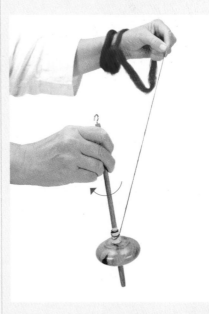

**9** Holding the spun yarn at about 90 degrees to the shaft of the spindle, rotate the spindle clockwise, storing the yarn until about 6in (15cm) remains. This yarn store is known as a "cop." Secure it to the spindle again. Repeat the process.

continued ▶

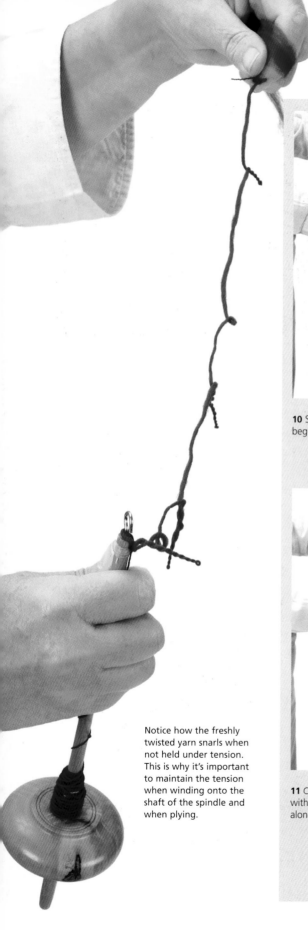

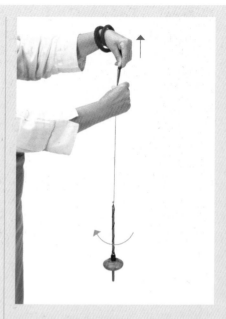

**10** Set the spindle in clockwise motion again and begin to draft.

**12** Draft more fiber while the spindle continues to rotate.

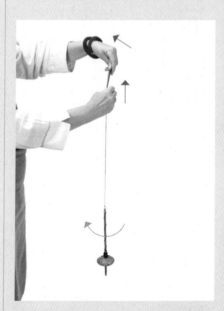

Notice how the freshly twisted yarn snarls when not held under tension. This is why it's important to maintain the tension when winding onto the shaft of the spindle and when plying.

**11** Continue to draft more fibers by pulling back with the left hand and sliding the right hand along the fibers toward the left hand.

**13** Concentrate mainly on the drafting and guiding the twist into the yarn, but keep an eye on the spindle ensuring it doesn't stop and start to reverse.

## Expert advice

**Plying from spindles**

You can use a spindle to ply just as you can spin. (Ply in the opposite direction, of course.) If you have at least three spindles, you can leave the singles yarn on two spindles and ply onto a third. Spindles can be mounted in a special rack or you can improvise by mounting them in a shoebox.

Often, though, you may not have spare spindles, so the spun singles need to be removed in order to free up the spindle for more spinning or for plying, and there are many options for how to do this. With a top-whorl spindle, you can normally just slide the cop of yarn off the spindle intact. Another good option is to wind a center-pull ball and ply from both ends (see page 66 for this technique using a wheel). Or simply wind each singles yarn into a firmly wound conventional ball and put each into a container so that they do not tangle on each other but run freely. A small pot placed upside down with the yarn feeding through a smooth hole is ideal.

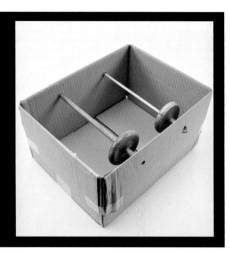

## Spinning with a top-whorl spindle

The principle of a top-whorl spindle is the same as a bottom-whorl spindle, but the design is different since top-whorl spindles have a hook to secure the yarn.

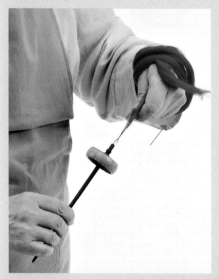

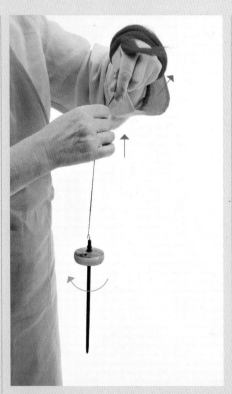

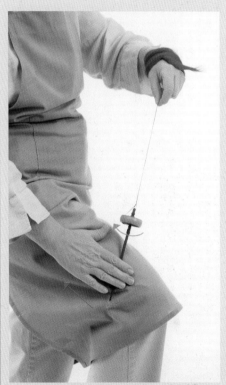

**1** You can start by creating your own leader by catching a few fibers in the hook and starting to spin. When you have enough, attach the leader to the shaft, twirling the bottom of the shaft clockwise while holding the leader at an angle of about 90 degrees, as for a bottom-whorl spindle. Alternatively, attach a conventional leader. Wrap fairly close to the whorl and then pass around the hook above the whorl, catching the leader into a groove in the whorl if there is one.

**2** Set the spindle in motion with a clockwise twist and start to draft. Keep the unspun supply of fiber out of the way by wrapping it loosely around your wrist and follow the method described in "Spinning with a bottom-whorl suspended spindle" (pages 46–47).

**3** Rotate the spindle with your fingers or, better still, roll the spindle along your thigh. Roll up the outside of the right thigh or down the outside of the left thigh for a Z- (clockwise) spin.

# Wheel spinning

SPINNING WITH A WELL-DESIGNED AND WELL-MAINTAINED WHEEL IS AN EFFICIENT WAY OF PRODUCING YARN. USING YOUR FEET TO PROPEL THE WHEEL LEAVES BOTH HANDS FREE FOR CONTROLLING THE SPINNING PROCESS, AND YOUR SPUN YARN IS AUTOMATICALLY STORED ON THE BOBBIN AS YOU GO.

## Preparing for spinning

Think about maintaining good position and posture. Your results will be better if you are comfortable during your spinning. Choose a comfortable chair without arms. Experiment with different seat heights if you have a choice—ideally your hands should be at about the same height as the yarn orifice on the wheel. Don't sit too close to the wheel—your knees should not be bent at more than a right angle as you treadle. Sit fairly square-on to the wheel. If your wheel has a double treadle (one where you use both feet alternately to treadle), you will automatically tend to do this. If you start to ache or slouch, stand up, stretch, and move around from time to time.

### Notes for beginners

It doesn't take long to become very proficient at treadling smoothly and rhythmically, but when you first learn to spin on a wheel it's easy to miss a beat and spin backward by accident, since you will have lots of things to think about at once. Without spinning at the same time, practice treadling slowly in a constant direction; practice both clockwise and counterclockwise. Try stopping and restarting without using your hands—you just need a single downward press if you deliberately stop when the rotation of the crank has gone just past the top of the stroke. If you stop when the rotation has gone just past the bottom of the stroke, you may be able to start by pressing down with your heel rather than the ball of the foot.

## Sitting at a single treadle wheel

Notice the hands are at a similar height to the orifice and that the posture is relaxed. The heel of the foot overlaps the pivot point of the treadle so that either the heel or the toe can start the wheel.

## Sitting at a double treadle wheel

With both feet on the treadles, sit directly in front of the wheel so that the hips are not skewed. The position should be comfortable so that you can spin without strain.

# Attach a leader

Try using a doubled leader so that it is easy to attach to the bobbin and has a readily available loop through for the straightforward attachment of the yarn as you start to spin.

**1** Take a generous length of existing yarn (about 60in/150cm), double it, and knot the end.

**3** Take the leader to the nearest hook and along the line of the remaining hooks ready to thread through the orifice.

**4** Pass the threading hook into the orifice and out of the hole on the other side. Catch the leader into the hook and pull all of the slack through.

**2** Pass the knotted end around the core of the bobbin on the wheel and pass the looped end of the leader through the two strands just behind the knot.

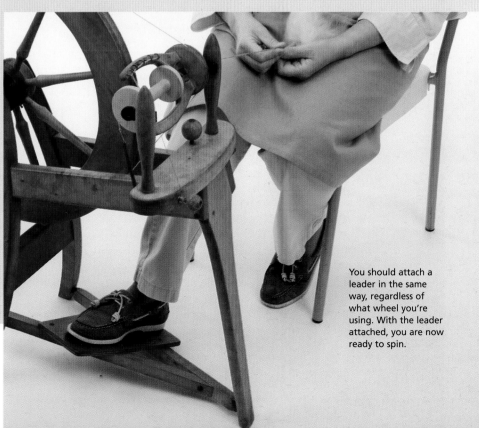

You should attach a leader in the same way, regardless of what wheel you're using. With the leader attached, you are now ready to spin.

Select the appropriate spinning ratio by changing the position on a variable whorl. On this type of wheel, align the belt on the drive wheel. The smaller the whorl, the higher the ratio.

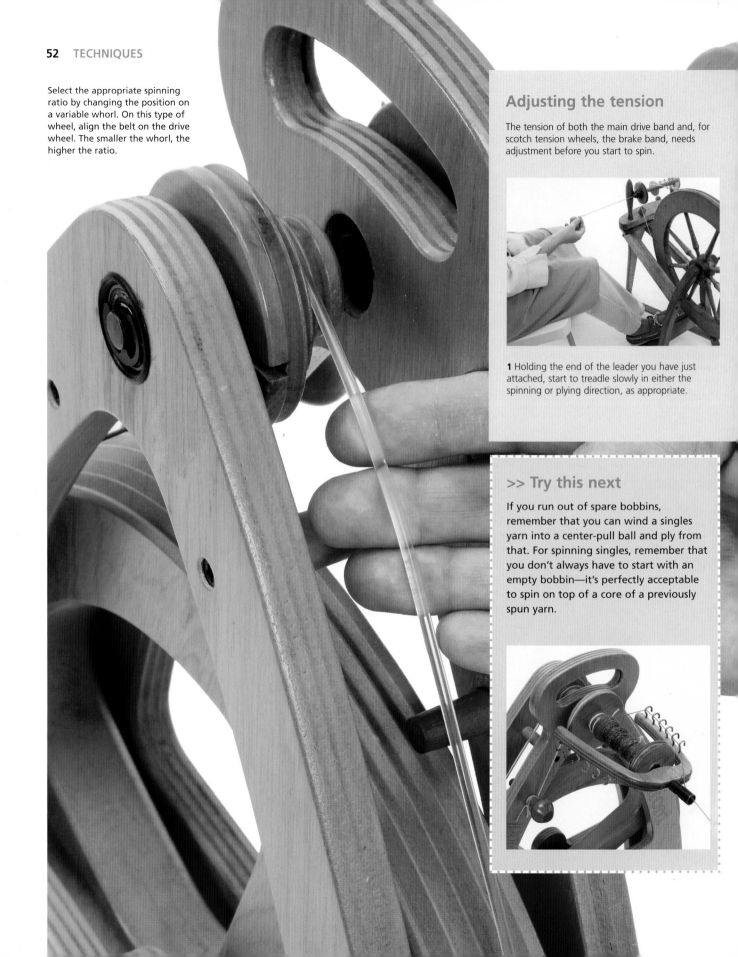

## Adjusting the tension

The tension of both the main drive band and, for scotch tension wheels, the brake band, needs adjustment before you start to spin.

**1** Holding the end of the leader you have just attached, start to treadle slowly in either the spinning or plying direction, as appropriate.

## >> Try this next

If you run out of spare bobbins, remember that you can wind a singles yarn into a center-pull ball and ply from that. For spinning singles, remember that you don't always have to start with an empty bobbin—it's perfectly acceptable to spin on top of a core of a previously spun yarn.

**2** If the drive band is slipping on the wheel or failing to make the flyer assembly rotate, increase the drive band tension until it is just enough to make the wheel rotate consistently. Feel the tension with your hand—it shouldn't be tight as a drum; just enough is the right amount.

**3** If the tension feels right but the flyer still isn't rotating, check that the flyer assembly is in good alignment and that no yarn or fiber is wrapped around the bearings.

**4** As you continue to treadle, you should feel a gentle pull on the leader—one that you can effortlessly hold back yet, when you relax, will allow the yarn to wind onto the bobbin. For scotch tension systems, increase or decrease the tension of the brake band until you feel a gentle pull. Do the same for a double drive band, adjusting the tension of the drive band.

## Starting to spin

You're now set to create some beautiful yarn. Refer to the sections on different types of spinning—woolen, worsted, spinning from the fold, etc.—to remind yourself what your hands need to do to spin these various types of yarn. They are all suited to spinning on a wheel.

**1** As you spin, the yarn will build up in one place on the bobbin according to which hook you are currently using or the position of the movable yarn guide. Your aim is to build up a nice even depth on the bobbin and not have steep hills and deep valleys, so you should change hook or move the yarn guide frequently.

**2** See how the yarn falls off the top of steep hills if you allow too much build up in one place. As you continue to spin and guide the yarn to the bobbin over the yarn that fell off, it will dig in deeply. If your yarn should break, the end is likely to bury itself and it could be very difficult to find.

**3** As your bobbin starts to fill, the tension is affected and you should readjust it from time to time so that you continue to spin under optimal conditions. If the yarn stops drawing in, stop treadling immediately and check the flyer assembly. It is likely that some yarn is caught around a flyer hook or around the spindle.

# Worsted spinning

THIS TECHNIQUE PRODUCES A YARN THAT IS SMOOTH, SLEEK, AND RELATIVELY DENSE; IT SHOWS OFF THE NATURAL LUSTER OF A FIBER. WHEN KNITTED, STITCH PATTERNS WILL BE CLEARLY DEFINED AND SHOW UP WELL, BUT A THICK KNITTED GARMENT WOULD FEEL VERY HEAVY IN THIS TYPE OF YARN.

The fibers are normally prepared by the combing method—whether you comb the raw fibers yourself (see pages 40–41) or start with a commercially prepared roving, sliver, or top. The short fibers are removed in the combing process and you are left with a parallel arrangement of longer fibers roughly equal in length. Luster and long-wools are normally spun worsted, and the technique can equally be applied to many other fibers. A version of the worsted spinning technique is also applicable to spinning certain types of silk: mawata (caps or squares) and silk brick (mulberry or tussah silk). The fibers in mawata silk will be extremely long, and a technique that shows off the luster of silk brick is just what is wanted.

## Basic worsted technique

The yarn you spin by this technique is designed to highlight the natural luster of the fiber and to produce a smooth, strong yarn.

**1** Prepare the wheel for spinning: set up a bobbin, adjust the tension to give a gentle draw-in, and add a leader if the bobbin is empty.

**2** Hold the prepared fiber in your left hand and, with your right hand, draw out a few fibers from the end. (The fiber used here is a pre-drafted roving of naturally colored alpaca.) Overlap these fibers with the existing spun yarn or pass them through the loop of the leader and pinch together. Start treadling in the Z direction.

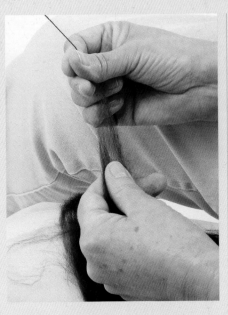

**3** Keeping the left hand stationary, and still pinching with the fingers of the right hand, pull forward a short distance (about 1in/2.5cm), evenly drawing out more fibers. The distance between your hands should be about the same as the fiber length.

**4** Slide the fingers of the right hand back along the newly drafted fibers, allowing twist to follow behind the fingers and smoothing the newly spun yarn as you go. You should see a triangular shape of unspun fibers held under even tension between your two hands. The twist at the tip of the triangle should give sufficient pull on the fiber supply to enable spinning an even yarn to continue.

## >> Try this next

With any given fiber, you can spin it relatively thicker or thinner according to the use you have in mind, and vary the twist angle (see pages 60–61). But do choose the fiber appropriate to the finished yarn and project you have in mind.

You can use a variety of fiber preparations such as a combed lock, roving, top, or sliver. Commercially prepared rovings should be opened up slightly by pre-drafting and/or splitting lengthwise into fingers.

Although normally associated with the spinning of long fibers, very fine yarns can be spun worsted from fine wools such as Merino, Cormo, and Bowmont, even though they are relatively short-stapled.

### Notes for beginners

- Start with the slowest spinning ratio on your wheel and, before you start actual spinning, practice treadling consistently and rhythmically in the same direction, stopping and re-starting in the same direction.
- Don't grip the fiber supply too tightly, otherwise it may bunch up behind the fingers of your left hand.
- If you cannot draft the fibers, your hands are probably too close together.

**5** After you have got into a rhythm and spun a couple of yards, pull a length of spun singles yarn (about 12in/30cm) from the bobbin and let it double back on itself. This is your reference sample, so keep it to hand as you spin and ply.

**6** Adjust the thickness (drafting more or fewer fibers) and/or the degree of twist in the yarn (treadling more or less in each section) to your requirements.

## Expert advice

### Correcting spinning thickness

A section of your yarn may turn out thinner, thicker, or more tightly twisted than you intended. If so, immediately break it off from the fiber supply and let it hang down loose from the orifice to untwist naturally.

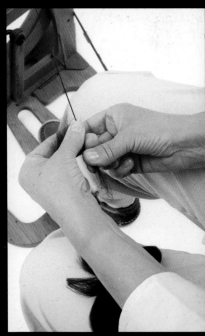

If too thin, overlap the start of the thin section with the fiber supply and continue from there. If too thick now that it's untwisted, you will be able to draft it out thinner before re-spinning that length and re-attaching to the fiber supply.

# Woolen spinning

THE TERM "WOOLEN SPINNING" REFERS TO A PARTICULAR TYPE OF YARN CONSTRUCTION AND FIBER PREPARATION. THOUGH A WOOLEN-SPUN YARN IS VERY OFTEN SPUN FROM THE WOOL OF SHEEP, MANY OTHER FIBERS ARE SUITABLE AND ARE OFTEN USED WITH A WOOLEN SPINNING TECHNIQUE.

The characteristics of a woolen yarn are lightness and loftiness in contrast to the smooth, sleek, and dense qualities of worsted. A woolen yarn will normally "bloom" in the finishing process, and woven items made with woolen yarns are often "fulled"; this is a type of felting finishing process.

Prepare fibers for woolen spinning by carding rather than combing, and then make rolags (see pages 36–37). Alternatively, you can spin a yarn with woolen characteristics directly from a carded batt made with a drum carder.

## Notes for beginners

You will hear terms like "true woolen" and "semi-woolen" applied to spun yarns. A "true woolen" yarn is one in which a carded fiber preparation is spun with a long-draw technique as described here. Both the fiber preparation and the spinning technique affect the yarn's characteristics, so a yarn spun short-draw but from a carded preparation is known as "semi-woolen." Similarly "semi-worsted" is a variation on a "true worsted" yarn.

## American long-draw spinning

With this technique, aim to create a woolen-type yarn with few slubs directly from the point of twist.

**2** Continue to spin slowly while drafting backward with the left hand. The advancing twist should be just enough to give an adequate pull on the fiber supply. Resist the temptation to compact the yarn with your right hand. This is largely a one-handed process and your aim is to spin a lofty yarn, not a dense one.

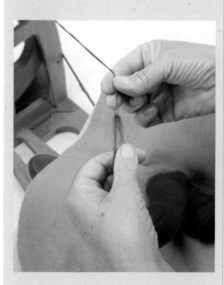

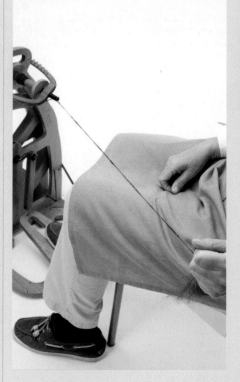

**1** Holding the rolag lightly, tease a few fibers from the end and pass through the loop of the leader. Spin to create a firm starting join.

**3** Once you have spun about 20in (50cm) of yarn, stop drafting from the rolag by pinching the end of the spun yarn. Correct any slubs by drafting them further, rolling the yarn lightly in your fingers to counteract the twist so that you can draft.

**4** Continue to spin without drafting until the length of spun yarn has sufficient twist and feed it into the wheel or store it on the spindle.

# English long-draw spinning

With this technique, exploit the fact that twist always jumps to the thinnest part of the yarn, allowing large slubs to be pulled out until the whole yarn is uniform in thickness.

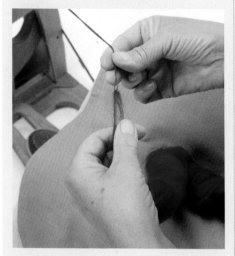

**1** Holding the rolag lightly, tease a few fibers from the end and pass through the loop of the leader. Spin to create a firm starting join.

**2** With your right hand, pinch the end of the spun yarn. Move your left hand a little farther back along the rolag and release the end portion for drafting.

**3** Still pinching with the right hand, spin to build up some stored twist behind those fingers. Briefly open and close the fingers of the right hand to allow controlled amounts of twist into the drafting zone.

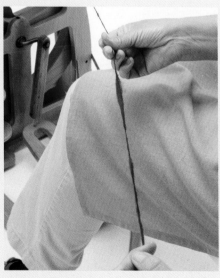

**4** You will see the twist jump to the thinnest parts, and you should now start to draft back with the left hand.

**5** Your drafting will only affect the thickest parts of the yarn—this is an elegantly self-regulating process. Continue until the drafted yarn is quite even along its length, adding a little further twist as you draft.

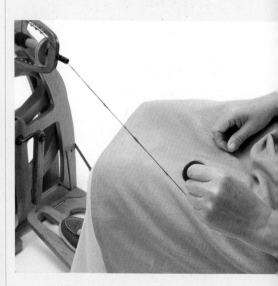

**6** Once the yarn is sufficiently drafted, continue to spin until it is sufficiently twisted, and feed it into the wheel or store it on the spindle.

# Spinning from the fold

THIS IS AN EXCELLENT TECHNIQUE WHEN SPINNING MEDIUM-LENGTH FIBERS FOR A SEMI-WORSTED RESULT. IT IS OFTEN DESCRIBED AS A SUITABLE TECHNIQUE FOR BEGINNERS. THIS MAY BE TRUE, BUT EVEN MORE ADVANCED SPINNERS WILL FIND LOTS OF USES FOR IT; DON'T TREAT IT AS PURELY A BEGINNER'S TECHNIQUE.

The semi-worsted yarns made with this technique will be slightly less dense than when spun with a true worsted method, which may just as easily be an advantage as a disadvantage. For example, if you are knitting a garment, you don't want the yarns to be too heavy because the garment will sag and, for a thick sweater, the sheer weight would be uncomfortable.

## >> Try this next

Roll the newly spun section of yarn to and fro between your fingers to give an excellent degree of control over the thickness of the yarn by using a small amount of temporary twist in the drafting zone. This controls how much or how little fiber is drafted at each stage.

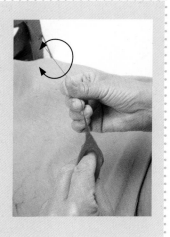

## Basic technique

This technique gives you a good deal of control over the fiber supply. The fiber supply is held at right angles to the direction of drafting, so the individual fibers fold over as they are spun.

**1** Pull off a staple length of prepared combed fiber, such as commercial top, and fold it over the index finger of the left hand. Gently pinch together the thumb and middle finger to hold the fiber in place.

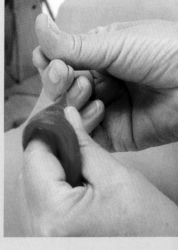

**3** While still holding the starting join, start spinning to add twist. Slide the front hand gently along the spun fiber for 2–3in (5–8cm) to give a smooth, worsted-like result.

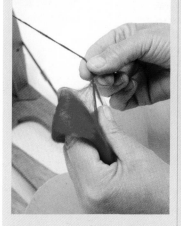

**2** Tease out a few fibers from the middle of the fold at the end of your index finger, pass through the loop in the leader, and fold over.

**4** Continue by drafting forward the same 2–3in (5–8cm) to make a further supply of fibers available for spinning, and repeat the process.

# Direction and balance

WHEN STARTING TO SPIN AFRESH, YOU HAVE THE CHOICE WHETHER TO ADD TWIST IN A CLOCKWISE (Z) OR COUNTERCLOCKWISE (S) DIRECTION.

It doesn't normally matter whether you spin your singles yarns Z or S, but once you start spinning in that direction you cannot reverse without removing the twist you previously added. When you ply, you add plying twist in the opposite direction from the original spinning direction (see pages 64–66). As you start to ply, you are not only twisting two spun strands together, at the same time you are undoing some, but not all, of the original singles twist, continuing until the yarn comes into balance. For a two-ply yarn, the balance point is reached when the number of plying twists per inch or per centimeter is two-thirds of the spinning twist, and for a three-ply yarn the ratio is three-quarters. But you don't have to be mathematical about it—let the two or three freshly-spun singles self-ply and they will naturally balance, giving a visual guide for how much opposite plying twist to add.

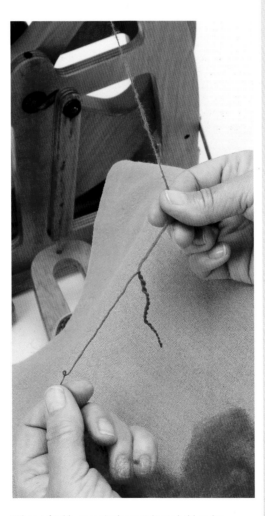

When a freshly-spun singles yarn is not held under tension it will have a strong tendency to fold back on itself and self-ply. Notice that an S-twist singles will self-ply in the Z direction and vice versa. The resulting plied yarn will then be balanced and will no longer have any tendency to tangle.

## Spinning/plying direction

Understanding S- and Z-spun yarns, and being able to spot the difference between them, is key to the principles of spinning.

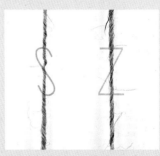

Spinning in either direction results in yarn where the twist looks like this. Notice that the line of slope goes either from bottom right to top left or from bottom left to top right. Notice also that if you turn the yarn (or this page) upside down, the direction of the slope is the same whichever way you look at it.

Plying in the opposite direction results in balanced yarn looking like this. The slope line mimics the slope of either the letter S or the letter Z, and so the convention universally used by both hand spinners and commercial yarn manufacturers for describing the twist direction is "S-twist" or "Z-twist."

# Thick and thin spinning

WHEN YOUR AIM IS TO SPIN A YARN THAT IS THICKER OR THINNER THAN WHAT YOU WOULD NORMALLY THINK OF AS "MEDIUM" (WHATEVER THAT MIGHT BE), YOU WILL HAVE TO MAKE SOME CONSCIOUS ADJUSTMENTS TO YOUR FIBER PREPARATIONS, YOUR SPINNING TECHNIQUES, AND, OF COURSE, MAKE SURE THAT THE FIBER YOU SELECT IS SUITABLE FOR SPINNING AT THAT GRIST AND FOR THE PROJECT YOU HAVE IN MIND.

## How much twist?
Look at this diagram of thin, medium, and thick yarns spun with the same twist angle:

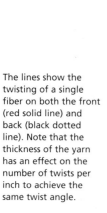

The lines show the twisting of a single fiber on both the front (red solid line) and back (black dotted line). Note that the thickness of the yarn has an effect on the number of twists per inch to achieve the same twist angle.

## Thick spinning
When you want to spin a thick yarn, select a low spinning ratio if you can, or spin quite slowly to avoid getting far too much twist into the yarn and feed the yarn into the orifice as soon as it is adequately spun. As there is not much time to fine-tune your drafting, it can help to work with fiber pre-drafted to almost the correct spinning thickness. Check frequently that the yarn is not getting over-twisted by allowing it temporarily to self-ply.

## Thick spinning
The intended result here is a chunky knitting yarn.

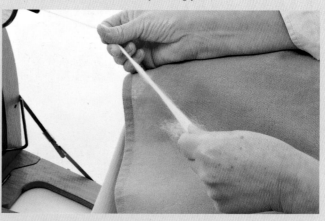

**1** The fiber supply needs only a little further drafting since it has been pre-drafted almost to the desired final thickness.

**2** The spun yarn is temporarily allowed to self-ply at frequent intervals to make sure that it is not becoming over-twisted.

## Thin spinning
For spinning a fine yarn, use a fine fiber suited to your end purpose. You may want to spin a fine yarn for lace knitting from a fine wool such as Merino or Corriedale, or spin a fine silk yarn for weaving. In each case you should partly pre-draft the fiber before spinning so that there is a little further drafting to be done during the spinning process, but not a great deal. You will then be in good control and you'll be in a position to concentrate on the uniformity of your yarn and on adding a sufficient amount of twist.

A fast spin speed is desirable to add lots of twist. If your wheel has a choice of different ratios, choose a high ratio for fine spinning. Special lace flyers and bobbins are available for some wheels, giving you a high spinning ratio and a bobbin with a thick core. If you have no choice of ratio, you can still spin finely, but you will have to do much more treadling for each length you

## Thin spinning

The intended result here is a fine yarn—for lace knitting or weaving.

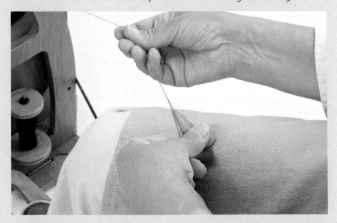

**1** Working with a pre-drafted fiber supply enables you to have good spinning control. Concentrate on drafting as evenly as possible and giving a sufficient amount of twist to your yarn.

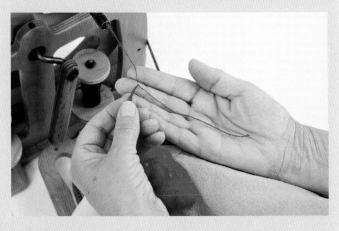

**2** Now do a self-ply test. If the plied result is firm, then your singles yarn has enough twist. If it looks too loose, add more twist and check again.

spin. And it's an easy matter to imitate a bobbin with a thick core by padding out a normal bobbin. The padding can be a short length of heating pipe insulation or some previously spun yarn with a layer of paper or fabric on top. If you are spindle spinning, choose a fairly lightweight spindle capable of fast rotation.

Fine yarn, highly twisted, has plenty of scope for getting tangled if you let it, and if your yarn breaks while spinning, it can be difficult to find the end, which can bury itself in the bobbin. So if your yarn should break, and you don't catch it before it disappears into the orifice, continue treadling and gradually slow to a stop rather than putting on the emergency brake. This makes it much less likely that the end will become buried.

*Notes for beginners*

• A thick yarn will build up on the bobbin very quickly, so be sure to change the hook or yarn guide position very frequently.

• If you are spinning on a wheel, make sure that the size of yarn will fit comfortably through the orifice. If it doesn't, consider spinning it on a spindle instead. Thick yarn will also have a greater tendency to catch on the hooks, the telltale sign of which is that the yarn stops drawing in. When this happens, stop and check the hooks before simply reducing the tension.

## Expert advice

**Skillful thick spinning**

Students are generally really surprised that they find it more challenging to spin thick than thin. Why would that be?

Referring back to the diagram of thickness and number of twists per inch (opposite), you'll see that a thick yarn has to be drafted very quickly in relation to a given rate of spinning twist being added in order to keep the number of twists per inch to a very low number. That means that you need a fairly firm tension to give a good rate of draw-in and your hands will have to work extremely rapidly to keep up. That also means that it's more difficult to maintain consistency when you are having to rush so much. The way to deal with this in a short-draw situation is again to pre-draft the fiber to almost exactly the final thickness you need to spin, leaving you with only small drafting adjustments to make. Then you use the wheel or spindle to add twist and store the spun yarn at a satisfyingly rapid rate.

# Spinning for evenness or texture

WHEN YOU FIRST START TO SPIN, THE IDEA OF BEING ABLE TO SPIN A YARN THAT IS SO UNIFORM IT COULD BE MISTAKEN FOR A COMMERCIALLY MILL-SPUN YARN SEEMS QUITE IMPOSSIBLE.

As you grapple with the spinning process, at the outset your yarns will very likely be (unintentionally) fairly lumpy and bumpy. But as time goes on and your consistency improves, you may find yourself yearning for a way to recreate those highly textured and highly desirable yarns that seem more difficult to master than even spinning.

## Evenness: spinning

Evenness comes from consistency of fiber preparation, consistency of drafting, and consistency of twist addition. So the more that an evenly spun yarn is your aim, the more important it is to invest the time into really thorough fiber preparation. This applies equally to the carding process for woolen-spun yarns, the combing process for worsted yarns, and any pre-drafting that you also carry out. Starting with carefully prepared fiber will give you the best possible start toward achieving an even result.

Try to get into a very even rhythm of how much fiber you draft at each stage and the rate of twist you add. A comfortable posture and relaxed frame of mind will all help toward this goal.

## Evenness: plying

Evenness of plying comes from carefully tensioning each of the single elements equally and guiding the plying twist into the yarn. As you start to ply, count how many treadles are needed to achieve the degree of plying twist you want in the yarn in a fixed length—the stretch of an arm, probably. (Comparing it to your reference sample.) If you continue to ply in multiples of the same length of yarn and count the treadles then, provided your singles yarn is consistent, you will get an even and consistently plied yarn (see pages 64–66).

## Texture

Texture comes in all different guises, starting with texture in the singles yarn. Think about the conditions described for evenness: the opposite conditions will give rise to textured yarns.

Starting with fiber preparation you can, for instance, card wool only very lightly, spin from a lightly teased lock not combed or carded at all, or deliberately add little lumps (called neps) to the fiber as it is being prepared (see below).

### Adding neps

Neps can be small knots of fiber, snips of existing yarn, or fragments of cloth.

Small lumps of fiber or small snips of existing yarn (neps) are being lightly carded with the main fiber to give a highly textured yarn. There is always a tendency for the neps to be shed, but a woolen-spun technique helps lock them into the yarn.

## Spinning a slub yarn

Irrespective of the fiber preparation, you can deliberately introduce thicker, and therefore less spun, parts of the yarn, called slubs. The key to this is to exploit the rule that twist will always migrate to the thinnest section of the yarn and that fibers held by twist at both ends cannot be drafted further.

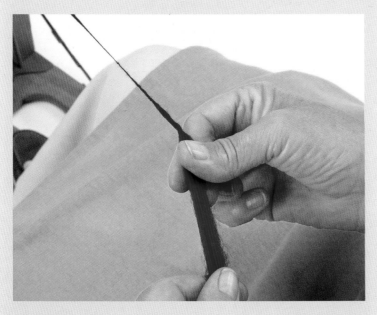

**1** With a worsted-related drafting process, spin a small section of regular thickness then move your drafting hand back and pull a thicker bunch of fibers.

**2** Move your drafting hand farther back beyond this thicker bunch and return to drafting more thinly.

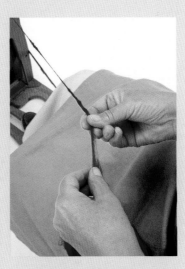

**3** Once twist enters the current thinner section, the slub will be locked and it will not be possible to draft it further.

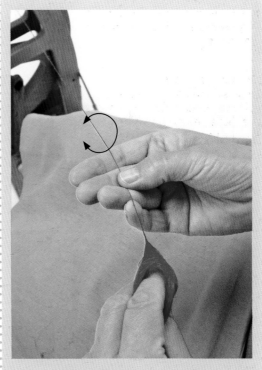

### >>Try this next

Rolling the last very short length of yarn between your fingers as you spin will add to or subtract twist from the drafting zone, and the effect of this is to increase or decrease the grip on fibers in the drafting zone. Only quite a small motion is needed to fine-tune your rate of drafting and get a really useful improvement when spinning for evenness is your goal.

# Conventional plying

YOU WILL NOTICE THAT A SINGLE STRAND OF SPUN YARN IS VERY LIVELY—CURLING AND TANGLING UNLESS HELD UNDER TENSION. IT IS ALSO WEAKER THAN A PLIED YARN AND, IF YOU KNIT WITH SINGLES, THE KNITTING WILL HAVE A PRONOUNCED SLANT. THEREFORE, YOU WILL GENERALLY WANT TO PLY YOUR YARN, WHICH MEANS TO SPIN TWO OR MORE STRANDS OF SINGLES TOGETHER.

Apart from certain special situations, you will twist in the opposite direction to ply compared to when you were spinning; so if your singles were Z-spun, you'll ply in the S direction, and vice versa.

Hand spinners probably make more two-ply yarns than three- or four-ply. A two-ply yarn simply means that it is made up of two individual single strands; it does not imply a particular thickness of the finished yarn. If you want a slightly thicker yarn, it is generally possible simply to spin thicker singles elements to create a thicker two-ply result.

The aim is normally to achieve a balanced yarn—this is one that has no

### Notes for beginners

Remember to treadle the wheel or twist the spindle in the opposite direction to the one used when you were spinning the singles. So if you treadled the wheel clockwise (Z-twist) when spinning, you will treadle the wheel counterclockwise (S-twist) when plying.

Threading the leader through the orifice (see step 2, right)

## Plying from two bobbins

To ply from two bobbins, you will need to support the bobbins so that the yarn can be evenly unwound.

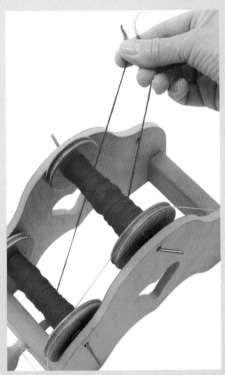

**1** Put the singles bobbins onto a lazy kate if you have one. If you don't have one, you can improvise with knitting needles and a shoebox.

tendency to twist back on itself in either direction. You can see whether a yarn is balanced by holding a loose loop of the finished plied yarn. This is a good guide if the singles yarns are freshly spun and then immediately plied, but there is a tendency for the singles twist to set temporarily if the yarn is left on the bobbin for a time. Then, even if you add the correct amount of plying twist, the yarn may still look unbalanced until the skein has been washed. Try keeping aside a small reference sample of freshly spun singles yarn that has been allowed to relax naturally into a two-ply yarn (see page 59). You then have a visual reference for how much plying twist to add so that the yarn will be balanced after the skein is washed.

## >> Try this next

You can ply together from more than two bobbins in just the same way. A three- or four-ply yarn has a rounder cross-section than two-ply, and enables you to make a thicker yarn when the fiber is unsuitable for spinning a thicker singles. A four-ply cabled yarn is made from two two-ply yarns plied together. Reverse the direction of twist at each stage (singles spun Z, each intermediate two-ply spun S, final ply spun Z), with the aim of balancing the final yarn. This means that the intermediate plying stage needs extra twist, which will be balanced out in the final plying stage.

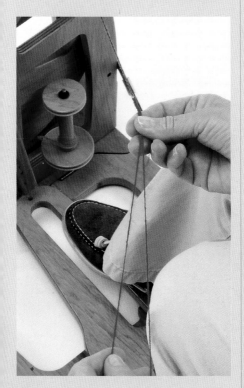

**2** Put an empty bobbin with a leader on the wheel. Thread the leader through the orifice and start to treadle (in the opposite direction to when you were spinning), holding onto the leader thread.

**3** Take the two singles ends, pass them through the loop on the leader, and double back. Hold them together as you start to treadle—the plying twist will then hold the join to the leader securely.

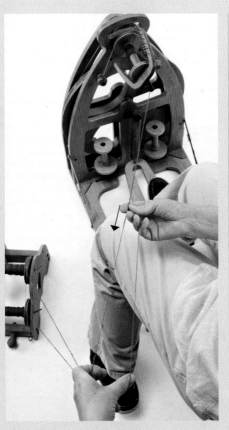

**4** Now hold the two singles about an arm's length back from the orifice under a little tension between the fingers of your left hand. Gently slide the fingers of your right hand along the yarn at a steady rate, starting from near the orifice and moving back toward your left hand, controlling the plying twist entering the yarn.

**5** When that length is plied, grip the yarn with your right hand and feed the yarn into the orifice, keeping the left hand in the same position and the unplied singles under gentle tension between the fingers, and repeat the process. You will need to move the yarn from hook to hook more frequently than when you were spinning the singles.

## Plying from a center-pull ball

This is a great technique for making a two-ply yarn from a small amount of singles without waste.

**1** When you have just a small amount of singles yarn to be plied, wind it into a center-pull ball using a ball winder or nostepinne (see page 79). If you don't have either, you can improvise by winding it around a smooth tube.

**2** Wind at a constant angle to the tube in looping movements, rotating the tube a small amount with each turn until the ball is complete, then slide it off the tube.

**3** Attach both ends of the yarn from the ball (coming from both the inside and the outside) to the leader just as when plying from two bobbins.

**4** Hold the ball in your left hand an arm's length back from the orifice with your thumb through the middle, and gently tension the two strands through the fingers of the left hand.

**5** Ply as for the two-bobbin method until the ball is used up, taking care not to allow a "plug" of yarn to escape from the middle of the ball.

## Expert advice

**Dealing with a break**

If one of the singles yarns breaks, don't tie a knot—just overlap the break and gently guide the twist until it is beyond the break. This is known as splicing. You can also help the process by rolling the join in your fingers.

# Navajo or chain plying

CHAIN PLYING IS A VERY GOOD DESCRIPTOR FOR THIS TECHNIQUE, ALSO KNOWN AS NAVAJO PLYING, AS IT INVOLVES ADDING PLYING TWIST AS YOU MAKE A CHAIN WITH LONG LOOPS—JUST LIKE AN EXTENDED CROCHET CHAIN.

The result is a three-ply yarn from just one supply of singles yarn. Three-ply yarn needs slightly more plying twist than two-ply would for the same singles yarn, and because the plied yarn is thicker, it will build up quite quickly on the bobbin. This is an ideal technique for when you don't need too much three-ply yarn and it saves on the need for extra bobbins.

## Basic technique

This is a great technique to master; it's especially useful for plying a color change yarn without mixing the colors (see pages 98–99).

**1** Set up the wheel with a doubled leader for plying in the usual way and mount one bobbin of singles yarn in the lazy kate.

**2** Start by feeding a good-sized loop of singles though the loop of the leader; fold it over the singles yarn and start to treadle slowly to make a three-stranded join with the leader.

**3** Place the single yarn in the crook of the little finger of the left hand, palm uppermost, and hold the open loop of singles using the thumb and middle finger of the same hand.

**4** Continue to treadle slowly and, with the right hand, guide the twist into the three-ply yarn being formed.

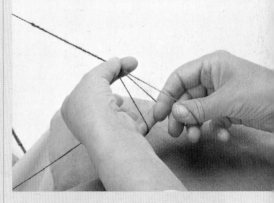

**5** Before reaching the end of the loop, use the middle finger of the right hand to reach though the loop and draw through another good-sized loop.

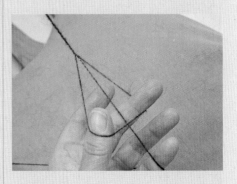

**6** Transfer the new loop back to the left hand and repeat the process.

# Andean plying

THIS PLYING METHOD ALLOWS YOU TO MAKE
A TWO-PLY YARN FROM JUST ONE SUPPLY OF
SINGLES. IT IS EQUALLY POSSIBLE WITH BOTH
A WHEEL AND A SPINDLE, BUT IT CAN BE
ESPECIALLY USEFUL WHEN PLYING FROM
A SPINDLE.

The principle is to wind a special "bracelet" of yarn
around your wrist that substitutes for a center-pull
ball, so that you can ply the two ends of the same
yarn supply together.

## Making the yarn "bracelet"

This technique is suited to a relatively small quantity of yarn,
otherwise it can be difficult to extricate the middle finger that secures
the bracelet while it is being wound. But using a hand as a spinning
tool has to be the ultimate in portability!

**1** Working from a bobbin or spindle of single-spun yarn, secure
the end by wrapping it a couple of times around the thumb of
the left hand.

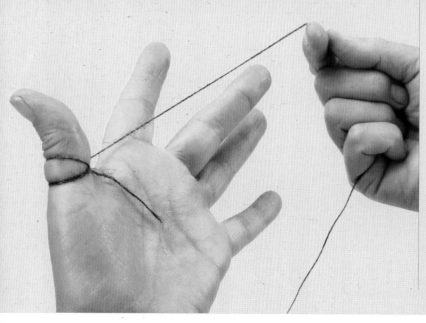

**2** Keeping the palm of your left hand facing you, pass the yarn
around the middle finger, take it back across the palm toward your
thumb, and right around the back of your hand.

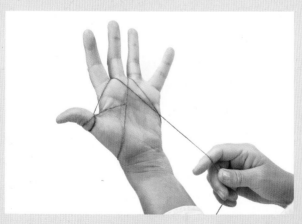

**3** Pass the yarn around the middle finger again, take it back toward
the non-thumb side it has just come from, and right around the back
of the hand again. At each stage you are looping around the middle
finger and then retracing your steps.

## Plying from the yarn "bracelet"

Now that you have your yarn round your wrist, the plying process presents no special problems.

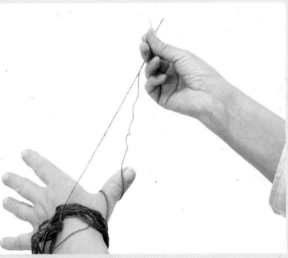

**1** Take both ends of the yarn together and start to ply as usual.

**4** Repeat Steps 2–3, maintaining only a light tension (you don't want to cut off your circulation!) until the singles yarn is all wrapped around your hand. Keep hold of the end of the yarn.

**5** Crook the middle finger of your left hand and slide the loops of yarn off the finger. You now have a loose "bracelet" of yarn around your left wrist.

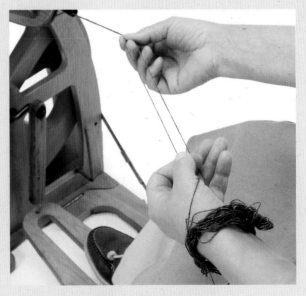

**2** The alternating loops that were previously around your middle finger are just enough to keep the bracelet holding loosely together and to keep yarn from tangling. You can think of this technique as plying from a center-pull ball, but without a ball!

# Fancy yarn plying

SPINNERS NORMALLY USE THE TERM "FANCY PLYING" TO REFER TO ANY PLYING METHOD THAT DIFFERS FROM AN EQUALLY TENSIONED BALANCED PLY OF EQUAL-SIZED SINGLES YARNS. IT COVERS A WIDE SPECTRUM, AND CAN GIVE A WONDERFULLY CREATIVE RANGE OF SUBTLE OR DOWNRIGHT OUTRAGEOUS SPECIAL EFFECTS.

Variations on standard two-ply techniques are achieved in a single plying stage, so they are no more time-consuming or troublesome to achieve than an ordinary two-ply yarn.

## Corkscrew yarn—using unequal tension

Holding one of the singles yarns under firm tension in your plying hand, guide the second one into the ply with very light tension. Notice how the result is a corkscrew effect. If you are working with two colors, the color under light tension will tend to predominate, and any time you like you can change which color to hold under more tension; this will give you a subtle change of color emphasis.

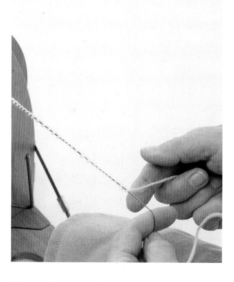

Ply together two singles yarns of different thicknesses for an even and attractive result, especially when the singles are of different colors. You can tension them both evenly while plying as usual, or accentuate the thick and thin characteristics by using unequal tension to achieve a more pronounced corkscrew yarn.

## Cable-plied yarn

Cable-plied yarn is achieved by a two-stage plying process, since a cabled yarn consists of two separate two-ply yarns plied together. The spinning and plying directions alternate at each stage of the process. For example: Z-spun singles, S-plied for the first ply, and Z-plied for the final ply. For this yarn to turn out balanced, the intermediate two-ply yarn must be intentionally unbalanced, with an overdose of S-ply. It may sound a very tricky thing to achieve, but actually it's not a problem.

**1** Look back at your self-plied sample of the singles yarn you kept for reference—that's how much plying twist you need to achieve balance. You know that you'll need to add more than that to achieve an over-twisted first ply, but how much more?

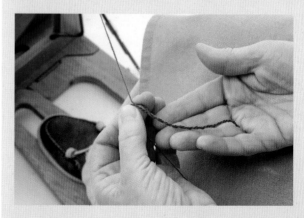

**2** Start the intermediate ply as normal but add some extra plying twist beyond the balanced stage—count how many presses of the treadle you make. Let the plied yarn relax and it will self-ply again into a four-ply yarn, but possibly a rather loose one.

## Bouclé yarn

This technique involves three different components: a core, a wrapper, and a binder. Bouclé is a loopy yarn (from the French word meaning "curly") and it is the wrapper forming the loops that will be the dominant element of the yarn. The core yarn must be fine, smooth, and strong, since it needs to withstand abrasion. If you use a singles yarn for the core, you should spin it in the same direction as the first ply so that it does not disintegrate on plying. It does not necessarily have to be handspun; a fine commercial plied silk or sewing cotton would fit the bill. The binder is a regular singles spun in the opposite direction to the first ply.

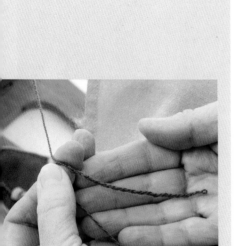

**3** Resume the tension and carry on treadling and counting. Keep inspecting the relaxed sample until it gives the result you want. Complete the overplied two-ply yarn, counting the same number of treadles for each similar length of yarn.

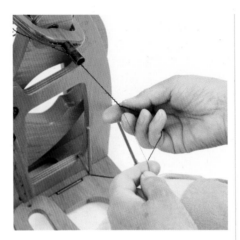

**1** Start to ply (in the opposite direction to the spin of the wrapper), holding the core under firm tension and the wrapper under loose tension, as for a corkscrew yarn.

**3** You must add enough plying twist so that the plied yarn is over-twisted. Check this by allowing the plied yarn to relax—it should self-ply in the opposite direction to the plying twist you are adding.

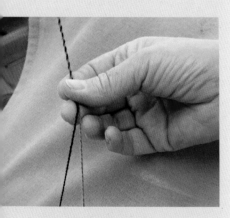

**4** Finally, ply together the two intermediate plied yarns in the opposite direction from the previous ply. Add twist until you get a balanced yarn, which will match the test result you obtained at the previous plying stage.

**2** With about 3in (8cm) wrapped, slide the wrapper along the core toward the orifice so that loops are formed. Treadle quite slowly, working fairly close to the wheel, and repeat the wrapping and pushing-forward motion, allowing the newly plied length to feed onto the bobbin each time.

**4** Ply once more with the binder thread, this time in the opposite direction to the previous plying direction. Keep both strands under similar tension while plying and aim for a balanced final result. Check this by allowing the plied yarn to relax—it should hang in a curve without any significant remaining amount of twist.

## Core-spun yarn

The principle of this yarn is to cover a core yarn completely with another fiber. The core provides only strength; it does not contribute visually to the finished yarn—so something like crochet cotton or plied mill-spun yarn is often used. The wrapper should be prepared pre-drafted fiber.

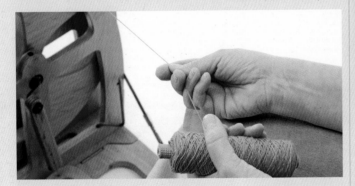

**1** Run the core yarn though the wheel to add twist to it in the same direction as it was plied.

**2** Attach the over-twisted core to a leader and start to treadle in the opposite direction to the twist just added. Join on the wrapping fiber and ply normally for a short initial section to secure it firmly.

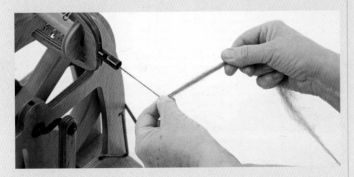

**3** Working close to the orifice, pinch the core and wrapping fiber together with the left hand and pull the wrapper at about 90 degrees to the core to draft it.

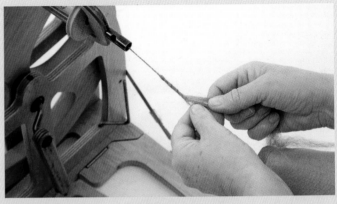

**4** Release the pinch with the left hand and, using the right hand as a guide, allow the drafted fiber to wrap the core, then repeat.

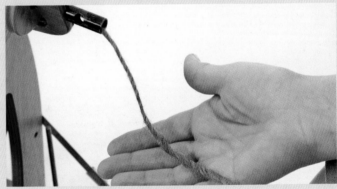

**5** You are aiming for the amount of extra twist added at Step 1 and the plying twist in the reverse direction at Step 3 to cancel each other out so that you are left with a balanced yarn.

### >> Try this next

You can achieve some wild and wonderful effects with core-spun yarns by using highly textured wrapping fibers and incorporating pieces of novelty yarns, shredded fabrics, and found objects. A large orifice is ideal for chunky art yarns.

## Bullion yarn

This yarn also needs a core, a wrapper, and a binder for its construction. Your core should be firmly spun with plenty of twist, otherwise it might disintegrate during the plying process. The wrapper should be a fine, unobtrusive yarn; its purpose is simply to prevent the bullions sliding along the core.

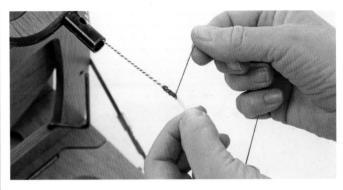

**3** Still working close to the orifice, and without feeding more plied yarn onto the bobbin, allow some wraps to overlap and build up into a "bullion."

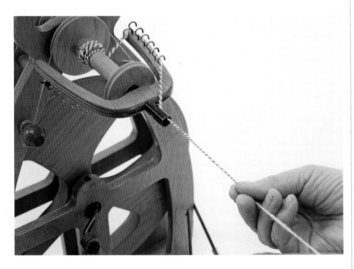

**1** Working fairly close to the orifice, start by plying together the core and wrapper normally for a short distance.

**4** Repeat a section of normal plying, make another bullion, and repeat, varying the spacing of the bullions. Throughout this first plying stage, add more plying twist than needed just for balance—this will be counteracted at the next stage.

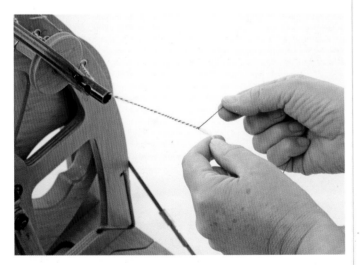

**2** Continue to hold the core in the usual position, but take the wrapper in the right hand and move it out to the right so that the wrapper is held almost at right angles to the core yarn and under slightly less tension.

**5** Ply together the bullion yarn with the binder in the opposite direction to the last plying stage. Aim for a balanced end result.

> **>> Try this next**
>
> Work with different color core and binder yarns, and change their roles from time to time to make bullions of different colors.

# Making a skein

YOU WILL WANT TO MAKE YOUR YARNS INTO SKEINS WHEN YOU TAKE THEM OFF THE BOBBIN OR SPINDLE SO THAT IT CAN BE WASHED AND BLOCKED, FOR DISPLAY AND STORAGE PURPOSES, AND TO FREE UP YOUR BOBBINS OR SPINDLES FOR MORE SPINNING.

A well-made skein is a thing of beauty, and can easily be achieved using a niddy noddy or other improvised methods. After your skein is washed, it's a good idea to attach a label recording basic details and the length. This is invaluable for project planning purposes (see page 132).

(see page 132)

## Expert advice

**Know your skein length**

**Measure the length of one circuit of the niddy noddy and count the number of turns as you wind the skein. Calculate the total length of the skein and record it on a label.**

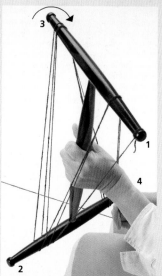

## Using a niddy noddy

The advantage of using a niddy noddy is that your skeins will be of a consistent length, appropriate for use on a swift later when winding into balls.

**1** Temporarily secure the end of the yarn coming from the bobbin to one end of the short arm at the top of the niddy noddy with a slipknot or clove hitch.

**2** Hold the niddy noddy by the central shaft and wind the yarn, going around the outer ends of the arms in turn, alternating from top to bottom and making complete circuits. Follow the arrows and numbers if you find this difficult.

**3** When the yarn is all wound, tie together the starting and finishing ends in a square (reef) knot.

**4** Add at least two figure-eight ties to the yarn while it is still under tension. It doesn't matter whether you use the same yarn or a different one for the ties. Pass them through the middle of the group of strands and tie securely. Remove the skein and finish as appropriate (see page 76).

### Notes for beginners

If you don't have a niddy noddy, you can still make a skein by winding around anything else you can find around your house—such as a large book, the arms of a chair, or the end of a table. Don't forget to add figure-eight ties before releasing it from the tension.

**5** To make a display skein, hold the loop under tension between your hands and rotate one end with the fingers until it is firmly twisted.

**6** Fold the twisted skein in half so that it self-plies. Tuck one end loop inside the other to secure it.

# Blocking

BLOCKING IS THE NAME GIVEN TO THE PROCESS OF
SETTING THE TWIST IN THE FINISHED YARN.

If the yarn is perfectly balanced, a damp skein can simply be left
to hang under its own weight to dry. But it's also useful to be
able to set the twist in a yarn that is unbalanced or to tame a
singles yarn temporarily. Weaving or knitting with energized yarns
such as singles has great creative potential.

## Blocking balanced or almost balanced yarns

The twist sets when damp yarn dries in a particular position—just like setting
human hair by letting it dry around rollers or drying curly hair straight. Once
dry, the position stays put. Avoid using too much weight otherwise the yarn
may become stretched rather than simply straightened.

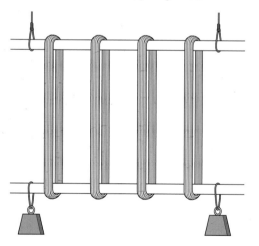

Above: Several skeins of the same
length can be blocked at one time
by suspending them between a pair
of dowels or broomsticks and
hanging weights, such as plastic
water bottles, from the bottom bar.

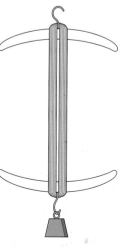

Right: A single skein can be blocked
by suspending it between two
padded coat hangers and attaching
a small weight to the lower one.

## Blocking singles or over-twist yarns

Active twist can be temporarily calmed by using steam, in the form of an
ordinary steam iron, to set it.

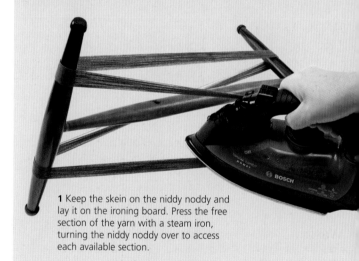

**1** Keep the skein on the niddy noddy and
lay it on the ironing board. Press the free
section of the yarn with a steam iron,
turning the niddy noddy over to access
each available section.

**2** With two hands, take hold of the cooled yarn
firmly and move it around the niddy noddy to
make the remaining sections of the yarn
available for ironing. Let it cool and dry
completely before removing.

# Washing and finishing

CHOOSE YOUR WASHING AND FINISHING PROCESS
ACCORDING TO THE TYPE OF YARN YOU HAVE CREATED.

If your yarn contains wool, remember that wool will felt under certain conditions; you can either embrace or avoid this effect. For silk, avoid very high temperatures and harsh treatment so as not to damage its lovely natural luster. Your aim in washing is to enhance the yarn's characteristics, keeping a worsted yarn sleek and smooth or allowing a woolen-spun yarn to bloom and enhance the loft.

## Washing wool spun in the grease

If you have spun with unwashed fleece, the main point of the washing process is to remove the grease (see page 30) and the dirt. Use very hot water and enough gentle detergent—either dish soap or regular shampoo—to give a lather. The amount will depend on how much grease is in the fleece. Let the tied skein of yarn soak for several minutes and then start to gently squeeze. The water may well be too hot for your hands—wear rubber gloves rather than cooling the water to avoid a thermal shock to the wool. Rinse in water of the same temperature. Repeat the process if the water is still dirty. A little fabric or hair conditioner in the final rinse will help to avoid static and promote a smooth yarn.

## Washing yarn from pre-dyed fibers

These fibers should be clean before you spin, but there could be residual dye that will bleed out of the yarn. In the washing process, check the color of the water, and rinse until it is clear. If there is a lot of color loss, don't plan a multicolored project that could be marred by colors that run into each other.

## Washing other yarns

You should be able to wash all of your plied yarns, though only a very little detergent is needed for clean fibers, just enough to act as a wetting agent. The washing process helps the plies to relax and improves the balance; it is also an important stage in the production of yarns spun by the woolen method as it helps the yarn to bloom when dry. Don't try to wash a singles yarn in the skein—the water will activate all the unbalanced twist and you can expect a mighty tangle! Wait until after weaving, crocheting, or knitting to wash singles. In all cases, handle the skein as if it were a loop of rope and try not to disturb it too much.

## Draining and drying

An old salad spinner is good as a spin-dryer for wet yarn. If you don't have one, simply squeeze out the excess water and blot in an old towel, then hang to dry. Hanging under its own weight will often be all that's required to set the twist.

## Steaming

Steam is hotter than boiling water and, when used with caution, steaming is a useful technique for setting the twist in a yarn, or for setting dyes for painted skeins and rovings.

You can use an old vegetable steamer over simmering water to steam a tied skein, a sample of yarn, or a dye-painted skein or roving placed inside a roasting bag. Five minutes would be adequate to set twist, about twenty minutes is required for setting dyes.

Steaming is also a good way to make sure a self-plied reference sample of yarn is fully balanced, even if the singles has been sitting on a bobbin for some time. But if you are tempted to hold the piece over a boiling kettle, please don't! The risk of a serious steam scald is just not worth it. The steam will successfully reactivate the twist and give you a true representation of balanced ply. If you are using a source of steam that requires the yarn to be suspended in some way, use long-handled tongs or, for a small piece of yarn, a pair of chopsticks.

When washed and dried, yarn can truly glow—just like this light green, lavender, and white 2-ply handspun yarn, made of hand dyed wool fiber.

# Winding balls

THE PURPOSE OF WINDING YOUR YARN INTO BALLS IS TO KEEP IT TANGLE-FREE, AND TO ENABLE THE YARN TO BE STORED IN A CONVENIENT FORM FOR DELIVERY TO YOUR FINAL PROJECT.

There are many ways of winding balls, and balls may be solid (allowing delivery from one end only) or with an open core, giving you the choice of working from the inner end, the outer end, or both at once.

### Notes for beginners

You can improvise the nostepinne method by using any other small, smooth cylindrical household item you may have to hand, such as a vitamin pill tube or spice jar. In fact, something with a snap-on lid is ideal to use for trapping the starting end of your yarn.

## Creating solid balls

You need to start with, or create, a solid core. A soft ball of felted wool about the size of a squash ball or golf ball is a good choice for a ready-made core. The ball should be firm, but not so tight as to stretch the yarn.

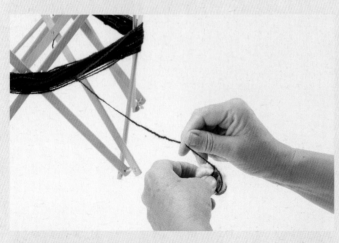

**3** Rotate the ball slightly, reposition the fingers, and continue to wind around the ball and fingers together for about ten turns each time, then repeat. Changing position frequently in this way avoids too much build-up in one place that could collapse and fall off.

**1** If you don't want to use a separate core, start by winding the yarn into a "butterfly" (figure-eight) around your fingers a dozen or so times. Remove the butterfly from your fingers and fold it over. The core shown here is a separate ball of felted wool.

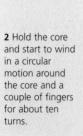

**2** Hold the core and start to wind in a circular motion around the core and a couple of fingers for about ten turns.

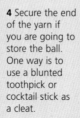

**4** Secure the end of the yarn if you are going to store the ball. One way is to use a blunted toothpick or cocktail stick as a cleat.

## Center-pull balls

There are excellent machines for winding center-pull balls that are easy to use, as shown here, and that produce very attractive and uniform balls.

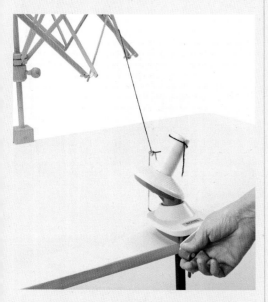

**1** Clamp the ball winder and the swift to a table. Feed the yarn through the yarn guide and lay it into the groove on top of the ball winder's cylinder.

**2** As you wind the handle, the central tube oscillates as it rotates and produces beautifully even and professional-looking results. Slide the finished ball off the machine and secure the end of the yarn around the outside of the ball by inserting a single twist with the end of the finger. Pass the end of the yarn through and tighten.

## Nostepinne method

An alternative to using a mechanized ball winder is to wind a center-pull ball using a simple device known as a nostepinne.

**1** Hold the nostepinne in your left hand, wrap the yarn around it a couple of times, and hold the loose end under your thumb. Wind in a circular motion at an angle of about 60 degrees to the shaft and, with each revolution, rotate the nostepinne very slightly so that each revolution lies next to, rather than on top of, the last.

**2** Slip the completed ball off the end of the tool and secure the end of the yarn around the outside of the ball by inserting a single twist with the end of a finger. Pass the end of the yarn through and tighten.

# Twist influence

The way you draw yarn off a center-pull ball affects the twist, and this differs according to whether the ball has been made using a ball winder or a nostepinne. This can easily be understood using a roll of toilet tissue as an analogy. Imagine standing the roll on the floor and pulling the end upward—twist is added. Turning the roll upside down and doing the same thing would add twist in the opposite direction. Pulling the tissue straight from a roll holder would neither add nor subtract twist.

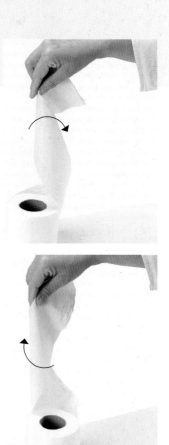

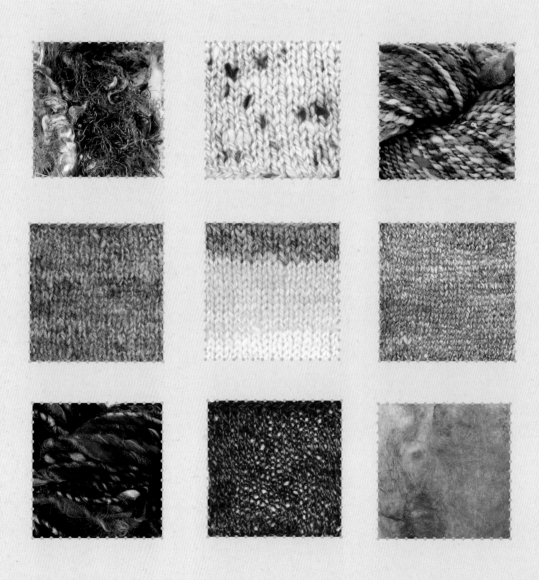

# Chapter 3

# Recipes

*This chapter shows a variety of yarn types with variations of each type. Each recipe gives suggested applications, fibers to try, relative cost, and durability. Each yarn includes a sample skein, the length yielded by a standard weight of fiber, and, when the yarn is suitable for knitting, a knitted swatch. Use the recipes as a jumping-off point for your own individual creations.*

# Soft knitting yarn

SOFT KNITTING YARNS ARE DESIGNED
TO BE SOFT AND AIRY. THEY FEEL LIGHT
IN WEIGHT BUT WILL BE WARM—IDEAL
FOR KNITTING.

You should use a woolen spinning technique to
prepare soft and airy yarns. The yarn will be
plied in the opposite direction from the singles
in order to achieve a balanced yarn—otherwise
your rectangular knitting will be skewed into a
parallelogram shape, and your garment may not
hang well or fit properly.

Swatch knitted on US size 5 (3.75mm) needles;
32 rows and 20 stitches measure 4in (10cm).

## Basic recipe: Pebble gray

**Cost:** Low
**Durability:** Medium

**Ingredients:** 2¼oz (65g) unwashed
raw fleece (1) or 1¾oz (50g) washed
and carded wool (2). The fiber used
was gray raw Shetland fleece.

**Quantity:** Makes 1¾oz (50g),
giving around 200yd (180m) of
finished yarn.

## Applications

Use soft yarn for the whole or the
major part of a knitted garment such
as a cardigan. Woolen-spun yarns
from soft fibers are comfortable to
wear and keep garments from
becoming too heavy. They should not
be used for hardwearing situations,
since pilling may be a problem.

**Knitting** Use as the neutral
background against which contrast
and fancy yarns can stand out.

**Weaving** Not suitable as warp yarns,
but may be used in the weft where
the fabric is intended to be finished
by fulling.

**1**        **2**

100%
Shetland
wool

## Top fibers for soft yarn

• Wool from fine-grade fleece with a short staple or prepared
wool top, which may be available ready-dyed.

• Luxury fibers such as cashmere, alpaca, and qiviut are
eminently suitable, though expensive, but could be blended
with a proportion of wool to good effect.

• Carded silk, such as throwster's silk, trimmed to a short
staple length, is also very suitable for a soft knitting yarn in
this technique.

## Method

**1 Making rolags** Make the wool into rolags
(see pages 36–37) and divide into two piles.

**2 Spinning** Spin each pile of rolags in the Z
direction using the woolen technique.

**3 Plying** Ply the two singles yarns in the S direction
until balanced.

**4 Finishing** Wind off into a skein, secure
with figure-eight ties, wash, and wind into
balls when dry.

# Frosted moss

**Cost:** Medium–high
**Durability:** Medium

**Ingredients:** 1¾oz (50g) rainbow-dyed throwster's silk (shown before carding [1] and after carding [2]).

**Method:** Card the silk, cutting the very long fibers as you go, to obtain an even staple length. Make the silk into punis and spin two bobbins in the Z direction using the woolen spinning method. Ply together in the S direction for a balanced result.

**Quantity:** Makes 1¾oz (50g) giving around 370yd (335m) finished yarn.

**1**          **2**

Swatch knitted on US size 3 (3.25mm) needles; 32 rows and 22 stitches measure 4in (10cm).

100% throwster's silk

# Bluebell wood

**Cost:** Medium–high
**Durability:** Medium

**Ingredients:** 1¾oz (50g) rainbow-dyed alpaca.

**Method:** Card the alpaca and make into rolags. Spin two bobbins in the Z direction using the woolen spinning method and then ply together in the S direction for a balanced result.

**Quantity:** Makes 1¾oz (50g) giving around 115yd (105m) finished yarn.

Swatch knitted on US size 6 (4mm) needles; 28 rows and 20 stitches measure 4in (10cm).

100% alpaca

# Crocus field

**Cost:** Medium–high
**Durability:** Low

**Ingredients:** ⅞oz (25g) each of prepared angora (1) and Blue-faced Leicester top (BFL) (2) and about ¼oz (7g) of lilac-colored Merino (3).

**Method:** To prepare each rolag, card together the wool and the Angora until they are well mixed. Then add a small amount of Merino and lightly card further before making into a rolag. Spin the prepared rolags onto two bobbins in the Z direction using the woolen method. Ply the two singles together in the S direction for a balanced result.

**Quantity:** Makes 1¾oz (50g) giving around 77yd (70m) finished yarn.

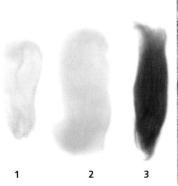

**1**          **2**          **3**

Swatch knitted on US size 7 (4.5mm) needles; 24 rows and 18 stitches measure 4in (10cm).

45% angora

45% BFL wool

10% Merino wool

# Lustrous worsted yarn

LUSTROUS WORSTED YARNS ARE DESIGNED TO BE SLEEK AND GLOSSY. THEY FEEL MORE DENSE AND SOLID THAN WOOLEN-SPUN YARNS. THEY WILL GIVE SHARP PATTERN DEFINITION AND HAVE LOW ELASTICITY.

The essence of a worsted yarn is that the fibers are totally parallel and each fiber is held under tension when spun. Therefore, they form a very compact yarn with little air trapped within the fibers. The yarn is plied in the opposite direction from the singles in order to achieve a balanced yarn. Any inherent luster in the fibers is shown off to the best advantage.

Swatch knitted on US size 5 (3.75mm) needles; 32 rows and 21 stitches measure 4in (10cm).

## Applications

Use worsted-spun yarn from long-stapled fibers in hardwearing situations and to showcase the natural luster of a fiber such as silk. They are typically resistant to pilling.

**Knitting** A fine-gauge worsted yarn might be ideal to show up the intricate stitch patterns of lace knitting, but a thicker worsted yarn could make a large garment feel heavy.

**Weaving** Suitable as both warp and weft yarns, plied, and as singles. Stripes of S- and Z-spun yarns will catch the light differently.

## Basic recipe: Bloody Mary

**Cost:** Medium
**Durability:** High

**Ingredients:** 1¾oz (50g) washed and combed commercially-dyed Merino wool.

**Quantity:** Makes 1¾oz (50g) giving around 140yd (130m) finished yarn.

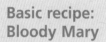

100% Merino wool

## Top fibers for lustrous worsted yarn

• Wool from lustrous fleece with a long staple.

• Prepared wool top from fine fibers, which may be available ready-dyed.

• Silk fibers in brick or top form, which may be available ready-dyed.

## Method

**1 Pre-drafting** Divide the top in half and pre-draft into fine rovings (see pages 38–39).

**2 Spinning** Spin each half in the Z direction using the worsted technique (see pages 54–55).

**3 Plying** Ply the two singles yarns in the S direction until balanced.

**4 Finishing** Wind off into a skein, secure with figure-eight ties, wash, and wind into balls when dry.

# Limoncello

**Cost:** Low
**Durability:** High

**Ingredients:** 1¾oz (50g) ramie top.

**Method:** Divide the top into two equal lengths. Spin each half of the top in the Z direction onto separate bobbins in your preferred worsted or semi-worsted method, pre-drafting or spinning from the fold. Ramie is best spun as a fine yarn. Ply the singles together in the S direction. Dye the skein using cold water fiber-reactive dyes.

**Quantity:** Makes 1¾oz (50g) giving around 180yd (163m) finished yarn.

Swatch knitted on US size 3 (3.25mm) needles; 36 rows and 24 stitches measure 4in (10cm).

100% ramie

# Cosmopolitan

**Cost:** High
**Durability:** High

**Ingredients:** 1oz (30g) natural brown alpaca top (1) and ¾oz (20g) red-dyed silk brick (2).

**Method:** Spin the alpaca and the silk onto separate bobbins in the Z direction using your preferred worsted or semi-worsted method. The silk will need more twist than the alpaca. Ply the alpaca and silk together in the S direction for a balanced result.

**Quantity:** Makes 1¾oz (50g) giving around 215yd (195m) finished yarn.

**1**          **2**

Swatch knitted on US size 5 (3.75mm) needles; 32 rows and 20 stitches measure 4in (10cm).

60% alpaca

40% silk

# White Russian

**Cost:** Medium
**Durability:** Medium

**Ingredients:** 2½oz (70g) washed very fine fleece, such as Cormo, Bowmont, or Merino.

**Method:** Prepare teased locks using mini combs (see page 41) and draw off into a fine roving. The remaining short fibers on the combs are waste, to be discarded or used for stuffing. Do not overload the combs by trying to prepare too many locks at once—a little goes a very long way in this yarn! Spin roughly equal amounts onto two bobbins in the Z direction using the worsted method, and spin as finely as you possibly can. You will need lots of spinning twist, so select a high ratio if you can choose. Ply in the S direction for a balanced result; you will similarly require much more plying twist than for a thicker yarn.

**Quantity:** Makes 1¾oz (50g) giving around 900yd (800m) finished yarn.

Swatch knitted on US size 0 (2mm) needles; 64 rows and 44 stitches measure 4in (10cm).

100% fine wool

# Spiral thick and thin yarn

SPIRAL THICK AND THIN YARNS ARE DESIGNED TO HAVE VISUAL INTEREST AND TEXTURAL CHARACTER OR, FREQUENTLY, BOTH. THEY MAY BE LIGHT AND BOUNCY OR FIRM AND DENSE, ACCORDING TO HOW THE PLIES ARE SPUN.

In a spiral yarn, one of the plies wraps around the other and gives a corkscrew-like textured effect, in both mono-colored yarns and where the two plies differ in color. The two plies can exchange their core and spiral roles from time to time. A thick and thin yarn, as the name implies, comprises two singles of differing thicknesses. The thick and thin elements can be plied into a relatively smooth yarn with a color contrast between the plies for interest, or a spiral yarn with thick and thin contrast—with or without color contrast—can be created.

Swatch knitted on US size 7 (4.25mm) needles; 22 rows and 17 stitches measure 4in (10cm).

## Applications

Use spiral thick and thin yarns for textural interest.

**Knitting** Use with plain stitches. The texture of the yarn will be predominant on the purl rather than the knit side of the fabric.

**Weaving** Suitable as weft yarns, especially as an accent against a smooth ground yarn. Probably not suitable in the warp due to abrasion in the reed.

## Basic recipe: Peppermint blue

**Cost:** Low
**Durability:** Medium–low

**Ingredients:** ⅞oz (25g) of two different-colored prepared wools. The fiber used here was white Jacob fleece, dyed pink (1) and blue (2).

**Quantity:** Makes 1¾oz (50g) giving around 77yd (70m) finished yarn.

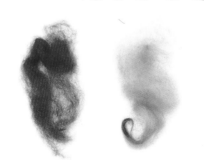

1                     2

## Method

**1 Spinning** Prepare and spin each color separately to a similar thickness in the Z direction using a woolen or semi-woolen technique.

**2 Plying** Prepare to ply in the S direction, holding one ply under firm tension, and the other quite loosely.

**3 Wrapping** Allow the looser ply to wrap around the firm core until balanced. If you wish, exchange the role of the plies from time to time.

**4 Finishing** Wind off into a skein, secure with figure-eight ties, wash, and wind into balls when dry.

100% wool

### Top fibers for spiral thick and thin yarn

• The same fibers as for soft knitting yarn for a thicker ply in a spiral yarn (see page 82).

• The same fibers as for lustrous worsted yarn for a thin ply (see page 84).

• Rainbow-dyed fibers as a contrast to a solid-colored base (see page 44–45).

# Lime twist

**Cost:** Medium
**Durability:** Medium

**Ingredients:** 1¼oz (35g) wool (1); ½oz (15g) brown alpaca top (2).

**Method:** Prepare the wool into rolags. Spin onto one bobbin as a medium thickness in the Z direction, using a woolen or semi-woolen method. Z-spin the alpaca more finely onto a second bobbin, using a worsted or semi-worsted method. Ply together in the S direction, holding the finer alpaca under tension and allowing the woolen ply to wrap around it.

**Quantity:** Makes 1¾oz (50 g) giving around 65yd (73m) finished yarn.

1          2

Swatch knitted on US size 7 (4.25mm) needles; 20 rows and 16 stitches measure 4in (10cm).

70% wool

30% alpaca

# Lemon sherbet

**Cost:** Low
**Durability:** Medium

**Ingredients:** 1¾oz (50g) washed and carded wool—1¼oz (35g) lime green (1); ½oz (15g) turquoise (2).

**Method:** Card each color of the wool separately and make into rolags. Z-spin each color onto a separate bobbin—the turquoise much finer than the lime green. Ply together in the S direction, holding each of the singles under tension for a thick–thin but nonspiral balanced result.

**Quantity:** Makes 1¾oz (50g) giving around 130yd (118m) finished yarn.

1          2

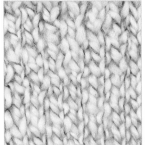

Swatch knitted on US size 6 (4mm) needles; 24 rows and 20 stitches measure 4in (10cm).

100% wool

# Ice cream sundae

**Cost:** Medium–high
**Durability:** Medium

**Ingredients:** 1½oz (45g) natural white prepared wool roving (1) and ¼oz (5g) rainbow-dyed silk top (2).

**Method:** Spin the wool roving in the Z direction using a semi-worsted method, aiming for a result that is not too dense. Spin the silk top finely in the Z direction onto a second bobbin, arranging the color changes as you prefer—splitting the top into fingers will give you quicker color changes than pre-drafting the whole top. Remember to add a good deal of spinning twist to the fine silk. Ply the wool and silk together in the S direction, holding the silk under tension and allowing the wool to wrap around it.

1          2

**Quantity:** Makes 1¾oz (50g) giving around 65yd (71m) finished yarn.

Swatch knitted on US size 8 (5mm) needles; 22 rows and 17 stitches measure 4in (10cm).

90% wool

10% silk

# Cable-plied yarn

Swatch knitted on US size 7 (4.5mm) needles;
22 rows and 15 stitches measure 4in (10cm).

THESE YARNS ARE DESIGNED TO HAVE VISUAL INTEREST AND TEXTURAL CHARACTER. THEY HAVE A VERY CIRCULAR CROSS-SECTION AND TEND TO BE RELATIVELY DENSE, SUBJECT TO THEIR CONSTITUENTS.

A cable-plied yarn consists of two two-ply yarns further plied together. It is, therefore, a four-ply yarn in total, and will be relatively thick unless the single elements are quite thin. The finished yarn should be well balanced, so the intermediate two-ply yarns must both have much more plying twist than that needed for a balanced two-ply. The spinning and plying twist directions are alternated at each stage of the process (see pages 70–71).

## Applications

Use cable-plied yarns for durable, textured results.

**Knitting** Fancy stitches will have good definition in a solid-colored yarn.

Multicolored yarns look good in plainer knitting.

**Weaving** Suitable as both warp and weft yarns.

## Basic recipe: Forest glade

**Cost:** Medium–low
**Durability:** High

**Ingredients:** About 1¼oz (35g) Merino in shades of green (1, 4, 5); ½oz (15g) natural gray Shetland wool (2), blended together (3).

**Quantity:** Makes 1¾oz (50g) giving around 66yd (60m) finished yarn.

70% Merino wool

30% Shetland wool

1    2    3    4    5

## Method

**1 Pre-drafting** Pre-draft the fiber and spin into a fine singles in the Z direction using a worsted or semi-worsted technique (see pages 54–55).

**2 Over-twisting** Wind into a center-pull ball, then create an over-twisted two-ply in the S direction working with the inner and outer ends (see page 66). Check there is sufficient over-twist by relaxing the plied yarn—this is how the final four-ply yarn will look and it needs to self-ply firmly enough (see page 70).

**3 Plying** Wind the two-ply yarn into a center-pull ball and ply both ends together in the Z direction until balanced.

**4 Finishing** Wind off into a skein, secure with figure-eight ties, wash, and wind into balls when dry.

## Top fibers for cable-plied yarn

• The same fibers as for soft knitting yarn for a softer result (see page 82).

• The same fibers as for worsted yarn for a lustrous cable-plied yarn (see page 84).

# River green

**Ingredients:** ⅞ oz (25g) each of dyed silk brick (1) and dyed wool (2).

**Method:** Spin each fiber in the Z direction, to a similar grist, onto separate bobbins. Ply the two singles together in the S direction, over-twisting well beyond the balanced stage, and wind into a center-pull ball. Complete the final ply from both ends of the center-pull ball. This method is helpful in avoiding waste left on bobbins during the several plying stages in a crepe yarn.

**Quantity:** Makes 1¾ oz (50g) giving around 77yd (70m) finished yarn.

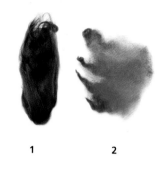

1    2

Swatch knitted on US size 7 (4.5mm) needles; 25 rows and 16 stitches measure 4in (10cm).

50% wool

50% silk

# Winter snowdrop

**Ingredients:** 1⅛oz (32g) dyed wool (1) and ⅝oz (18g) silk brick (2).

**Method:** This yarn has one ply of silk and three of wool. The first plying stage requires one 2-ply of wool; the other a silk/wool combination. Ply the combination first, then the remaining wool can be plied from a center-pull ball. The final combination is plied from two bobbins. The singles are all Z-spun; the intermediate over-twisted ply is in the S direction and the final balancing ply in the Z direction.

1    2

**Quantity:** Makes 1¾oz (50g) giving around 77yd (70m) finished yarn.

Swatch knitted on US size 6 (4mm) needles; 26 rows and 17 stitches measure 4in (10cm).

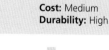

64% wool

36% silk

# Deadly nightshade

**Ingredients:** 1½oz (45g) prepared dyed Merino (1 and 2) and ¼oz (5g) natural tussah silk brick (3).

**Method:** First, Z-spin all the silk onto one bobbin using a worsted or semi-worsted technique, using plenty of twist for the silk. Next, Z-spin one of the Merino colors onto a second bobbin. Ply the Merino with the silk in the S direction, remembering to add over-twist at this intermediate stage. About half the silk should be left over. Repeat the process, spinning the second color of Merino and plying with the remaining silk with over-twist. The final balanced combination is plied from the two bobbins of two-ply. The

1    2    3

recommended order of work here needs only three bobbins in total, but if you spin both bobbins of Merino before plying the first one with the silk, you will need four.

**Quantity:** Makes 1¾oz (50g) giving around 77yd (70m) finished yarn.

Swatch knitted on US size 7 (4.5mm) needles; 25 rows and 16 stitches measure 4in (10cm).

90% Merino

10% silk

# Color-blended yarn

COLOR-BLENDED YARNS ARE DESIGNED FOR VISUAL EFFECT BY BLENDING DIFFERENT COLORS OF FIBERS BEFORE SPINNING.

The colors may all be blended thoroughly for an optical color mix, just like mixing paint colors, or a special color transition may be planned. To retain distinct color separations at the plying stage, prepare all of the fiber blends first, divide into two halves, and spin each half in the same order.

Swatch knitted on US size 6 (4mm) needles; 28 rows and 18 stitches measure 4in (10cm).

## Applications

Use color-blended yarns where their visual effects are desirable.

**Knitting** With a very gradual color transition, solid-colored areas of knitting enable fancy stitches to show up well. More random blends work better with plainer knitting.

**Weaving** Suitable as both warp and weft yarns, depending on the spinning method used.

## Basic recipe: Marshmallow pink

**Cost:** Medium–low
**Durability:** Medium

**Ingredients:** The wool used here was a top of commercially-dyed Merino (pink (1) and magenta (2)), a top of Blue-faced Leicester (BFL) (natural white) (3), and a top of Shetland (natural gray) (4). Use 1¾oz (50g) prepared wool in total.

**Quantity:** Makes 1¾oz (50g) giving around 120yd (110m) finished yarn.

50% Merino wool

25% BFL wool

25% Shetland wool

1      2      3      4

## Top fibers for color-blend yarn

• The same fibers as for soft knitting yarn for a soft yarn (see page 82).

• The same fibers as for worsted yarn for a lustrous result (see page 84).

## Method

**1 Preparing rolags** Create a set of rolags, starting with one single color, then adding increasing proportions of the next color and reducing the proportion of the first (see pages 36–37). Progress in the same way through all the colors. Line up the rolags in order and divide each rolag in half.

**2 Spinning bobbins** Spin two separate bobbins in the Z direction using a woolen or semi-woolen technique (see pages 56–57). Make sure the rolags are spun in exactly the same order for each bobbin.

**3 Plying** Ply together normally in the S direction until balanced. If the color transitions do not exactly coincide, you will get a "barber pole" effect at that point. If you prefer to avoid that, break off a length of one of the singles to realign the color change and make a spliced join (see page 66).

**4 Finishing** Wind off into a skein, secure with figure-eight ties, wash, and wind into balls when dry.

# Blueberry crush

**Cost:** Medium
**Durability:** Medium

**Ingredients:** 1¾oz (50g) total of mohair, in natural white (1), blue (2), and dark green (3). They can be a combination of clean locks and prepared top.

**Method:** Follow the basic recipe method, preparing a shaded range of rolags, dividing each in half and spinning two separate bobbins in the Z direction in the same color order. Ply the singles together in the S direction, matching up the colors as you go.

**Quantity:** Makes 1¾oz (50g) giving around 100yd (90m) finished yarn.

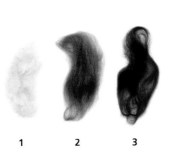

1     2     3

Swatch knitted on US size 5 (3.75mm) needles; 25 rows and 20 stitches measure 4in (10cm).

100% mohair

# Wild bramble

**Cost:** Medium
**Durability:** Medium–low

**Ingredients:** ¾oz (20g) natural bamboo top (1) and about 1oz (30g) total of Merino top in several shades of pink (2–6).

**Method:** Arrange the pink tops in a shaded color order and, starting with the first color, blend the bamboo and Merino on hand cards and form into a rolag. Repeat, using less of the first pink and a little of the second in the next blend, continuing to blend around the same amount of bamboo in each case. Divide each rolag in half and follow the basic method of spinning and plying.

1   2   3   4   5   6

**Quantity:** Makes 1¾oz (50g) giving around 150yd (135m) finished yarn.

Swatch knitted on US size 5 (3.75mm) needles; 29 rows and 22 stitches measure 4in (10cm).

60% Merino wool

40% bamboo

# Pistachio

**Cost:** Low
**Durability:** Medium–high

**Ingredients:** 1¾oz (50g) total of cotton sliver—a combination of natural (1) and blue (2), green (3), and turquoise (4), dyed with fiber-reactive dyes.

**Method:** Use fine hand cards for blending the colors of the cotton, and form into punis. Follow the method in the basic recipe for creating a shaded set of punis, divided in half before spinning long-draw in the Z direction and creating a balanced S-ply.

**Quantity:** Makes 1¾oz (50g) giving around 440yd (400m) finished yarn.

1     2     3     4

Swatch knitted on US size 5 (3.75mm) needles; 52 rows and 38 stitches measure 4in (10cm).

100% cotton

# Flecked yarn

FLECKED YARNS ARE DESIGNED TO GIVE
VISUAL INTEREST BY BLENDING SMALL
AMOUNTS OF DIFFERENT "NEPS" INTO
THE MAIN FIBER SUPPLY BEFORE SPINNING,
GIVING A "HEATHERED" EFFECT.

Swatch knitted on US size 7 (4.5mm) needles;
24 rows and 15 stitches measure 4in (10cm).

You will normally spin these yarns using a
woolen-spun method, the materials for the
"neps" being blended just sufficiently into the
main fiber supply in the carding process. You
can use a wide variety of materials for the
flecks, which can give lots of texture as well as
color contrast. The woolen spinning method
helps to lock the short flecks into the yarn.

## Applications

Use flecked yarns for textural
interest.

**Knitting** Multicolored yarns show to
better advantage in plain knitting.

Fancy stitches may show up less clearly
than with a solid-colored yarn.

**Weaving** Suitable as weft yarns.

## Basic recipe:
## Raspberry ripple

**Cost:** Low
**Durability:** Medium

**Ingredients:** 1¾oz (50g) prepared
natural wool and a small amount of
existing yarn snipped into tiny pieces.
The wool used here was a top of
Blue-faced Leicester (natural white)
(1); the contrast flecks came from a
previously handspun woolen yarn (2).

**Quantity:** 1¾oz (50g) giving around
65yd (59m) finished yarn.

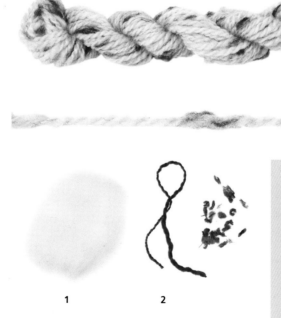

1                    2

## Method

**1 Carding** Card the wool on its own first, using
either hand cards or a drum carder. Add the
flecks and lightly card further. Make into rolags.

**2 Spinning bobbins** Spin two equal bobbins
in the Z direction using a woolen or semi-woolen
technique (see pages 56–57).

**3 Plying** Ply together normally in the S direction
until balanced.

**4 Finishing** Wind off into a skein, secure
with figure-eight ties, wash, and wind into balls
when dry.

95% wool

5% existing
yarn

## Top fibers for flecked yarn

• The same fibers as for soft knitting yarn for the main fiber (see
page 82).

• A wide variety of contrast fibers or yarns that will adhere
sufficiently to the main fiber for the flecks.

# Cherry blush

**Cost:** Low
**Durability:** Medium–high

**Ingredients:** 1oz (30g) natural gray Shetland top (1), ¾oz (22g) bleached linen top (2), and a very small amount of pink Merino top (3).

**Method:** Card the wool and linen together quite thoroughly before snipping tiny amounts of pink Merino with scissors onto the mix. Make a couple of further strokes before making into rolags. Spin the rolags in the Z direction using a woolen or semi-woolen method and ply for a balanced result as usual in the S direction. The linen in this mix provides a firm key to hold the short lengths of fleck fibers in place.

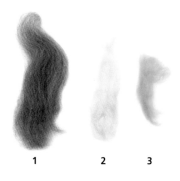

**1**       **2**       **3**

**Quantity:** Makes 1¾oz (50g) giving around 120yd (110m) finished yarn.

Swatch knitted on US size 5 (3.75mm) needles; 28 rows and 20 stitches measure 4in (10cm).

60% Shetland wool

38% linen

2% Merino wool

# Banana split

**Cost:** Medium
**Durability:** Medium–low

**Ingredients:** 1¾oz (50g) natural soy fiber top (1) and a small amount of green rough-spun linen yarn (2).

**Method:** Card the soy top using fine hand cards, then, with some fiber on each card, snip very small pieces of linen yarn on top. Card a little more to bed the linen pieces into the fiber batt, then form into small rolags or punis. Spin as usual in the Z direction and ply in the S direction for a balanced result.

**Quantity:** Makes 1¾oz (50g) giving around 200yd (180m) finished yarn.

**1**          **2**

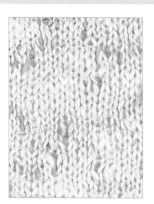

Swatch knitted on US size 3 (3.25mm) needles; 36 rows and 24 stitches measure 4in (10cm).

95% soy

5% linen

# Blueberry cheesecake

**Cost:** Low
**Durability:** Medium–high

**Ingredients:** 1oz (30g) natural Blue-faced Leicester top (1), about ¾oz (20g) linen top (2), and a small amount of purple Merino top (3).

**Method:** Follow the method for "Cherry blush," blending the wool and linen tops thoroughly first, then adding the snipped Merino.

**Quantity:** Makes 1¾oz (50g) giving around 120yd (110m) finished yarn.

**1**       **2**       **3**

Swatch knitted on US size 5 (3.75mm) needles; 28 rows and 20 stitches measure 4in (10cm).

60% wool

40% linen

# Slub yarn

THESE YARNS ARE DESIGNED TO GIVE
TEXTURAL INTEREST BY INCORPORATING
INTENTIONAL THICK PLACES, CALLED
"SLUBS," INTO THE SINGLES.

You will normally use a fairly short-stapled fiber
for slub yarns, spinning the singles with a
modification of the woolen-spun method. You
will ply the yarn normally for strength, and in
order to avoid the chance of thick slubs from
both singles coinciding, you may opt to ply just
one slubbed singles with a second smooth ply
matching the regular thickness of the first. As a
beginner you should embrace the slubs that you
produce unintentionally at first—you may find it
trickier to reproduce them by design later on.

Swatch knitted on US size 5 (3.75mm)
needles; 28 rows and 20 stitches measure
4in (10cm).

## Applications

Use slub yarns for visual or
textural interest.

**Knitting** Textured yarns show to
better advantage in plain knitting,
especially on the purl side of the
fabric. Fancy stitches may show up
less clearly than with a smooth yarn.

**Weaving** Suitable as weft yarns.
May be strong enough for warp,
but the slubs may not pass easily
through the heddles or the reed.

## Basic recipe:
## Caffé latte

**Cost:** Low
**Durability:** Medium–low

**Ingredients:** 1¾oz (50g) natural
cotton top. The cotton top used here
contained two natural colors— pale
olive green (1) and ecru (2).

**Quantity:** Makes 1¾oz (50g) giving
around 190yd (180m) finished yarn.

100%
cotton

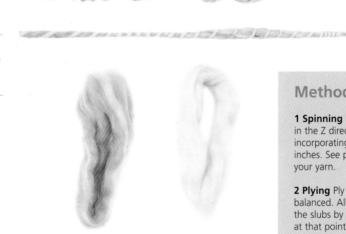

1                    2

## Method

**1 Spinning bobbins** Spin two equal bobbins
in the Z direction using a semi-woolen technique,
incorporating slubs on one bobbin only every few
inches. See page 63 for how to spin slubs into
your yarn.

**2 Plying** Ply together in the S direction until
balanced. Allow the non-slub ply to wrap around
the slubs by altering the angle of twist manually
at that point.

**3 Finishing** Wind off into a skein, secure
with figure-eight ties, wash, and wind into balls
when dry.

### Top fibers for slub yarn

• Short-stapled wools such as Down breeds.

• Fibers with inherent texture, such as throwster's silk.

• Short-stapled cellulose fibers such as cotton.

# Cappuccino

**Ingredients:** 1¾oz (50g) carded linen/silk-blended short-stapled fiber.

**Method:** Card the fiber on fine hand cards and make into punis. Start spinning in the Z direction using a woolen spinning technique and incorporate slubs at intervals. This fiber lends itself to textured but fine spinning, so it will need a lot of twist. Spin two separate bobbins, one slubbed and one regular, and ply according to the basic recipe.

**Quantity:** Makes 1¾oz (50g) giving around 265yd (240m) finished yarn.

Swatch knitted on US size 3 (3.25mm) needles; 30 rows and 24 stitches measure 4in (10cm).

60% linen

40% silk

# Freckled egg

**Ingredients:** 1⅛oz (30g) natural (1) and ⅝ oz (20g) navy blue (2) tussah silk tops.

**Method:** Spin one bobbin of natural in the Z direction using a semi-worsted method, making slubs at intervals. Spin the navy in the Z direction using the same method onto a separate bobbin, but without slubs. Ply together in the S direction, wrapping the slubs.

**Quantity:** Makes 1¾oz (50g) giving around 260yd (235m) finished yarn.

**1**          **2**

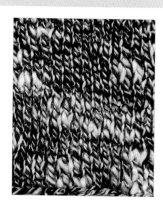

Swatch knitted on US size 3 (3.25mm) needles; 38 rows and 24 stitches measure 4in (10cm).

100% silk

# Amber

**Ingredients:** 1oz (28g) Merino tops in various shades of yellow (1) and about ¾oz (21g) natural ramie top (2).

**Method:** Spin one bobbin of Merino in the Z direction using a semi-worsted method, making slubs at intervals. Spin a separate bobbin of ramie in the Z direction using a worsted or semi-worsted technique. Ply together in the S direction, wrapping the slubs.

**Quantity:** Makes 1¾oz (50g) giving around 180yd (165m) finished yarn.

**1**          **2**

Swatch knitted on US size 5 (3.75mm) needles; 32 rows and 20 stitches measure 4in (10cm).

57% Merino wool

43% ramie

# Three-ply chunky yarn

THREE-PLY CHUNKY YARNS ARE PRINCIPALLY DESIGNED TO BE FATTER FOR CHUNKIER KNITTING. USING THREE PLIES RATHER THAN TWO IS A GOOD WAY TO ACHIEVE THIS.

You should choose your fibers and spinning method according to the project you have in mind—from purely woolen to purely worsted and anything in between. The yarn is plied in the opposite direction from which the three singles were spun in order to achieve a balanced yarn. Compared to a two-ply yarn, use slightly less twist in the singles. Three plies give a lovely rounded cross-section to the yarn.

Swatch knitted on US size 6 (4mm) needles; 16 rows and 10 stitches measure 4in (10cm).

## Applications

Use three-ply chunky yarn for the whole or the major part of a knitted garment such as a bulky pullover or cardigan. The three plies give strength and consistency to the yarn.

**Knitting** Use for warm garments or attractive home accessories such as pillows. Think about weight and wear considerations for a garment, and choose your spinning method accordingly.

**Weaving** May be used as weft and, subject to a suitable reed that will accommodate a thick yarn, may also be used as warp.

## Basic recipe: Glacier white

**Cost:** Low
**Durability:** Medium–high

**Ingredients:** 1¾oz (50g) prepared wool. The fiber used here was a natural white wool roving.

**Quantity:** Makes 1¾oz (50g) giving around 37yd (34m) finished yarn.

100% wool

## Top fibers for three-ply chunky yarn

• Wool from medium or short-stapled fleece is always suitable.

• Luxury fibers such as cashmere, alpaca, and qiviut are eminently suitable, though expensive, but could be blended with a proportion of wool to good effect.

• Carded silk, such as throwster's silk trimmed to a short staple length, is also very suitable for a soft knitting yarn in this technique.

## Method

**1 Preparation** Divide the wool into three equal portions.

**2 Spinning bobbins** Spin each portion onto a separate bobbin in the S direction using the worsted or semi-worsted technique (see pages 54–55). (Note that the usual S and Z directions are reversed in this yarn as the roving had a light Z-twist present and needed to be S-spun so that it could be drafted.)

**3 Plying** Ply the three singles yarns in the Z direction until balanced.

**4 Finishing** Wind off into a skein, secure with figure-eight ties, wash, and wind into balls when dry.

# Fall leaves

**Ingredients:** 1¼oz (35g) natural gray Shetland top (1) and ¼oz (7g) each of brown and green Merino top, shown after blending with the gray (2 and 3).

**Method:** Divide the main wool into thirds, with one more generous portion. Blend each of the other portions with one of the additional colors. Make into rolags and spin each color in the Z direction onto separate bobbins. Ply the three together in the S direction.

**Quantity:** Makes 1¾oz (50g) giving around 100yd (90m) finished yarn.

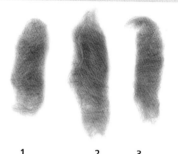

1    2    3

Swatch knitted on US size 10½ (6.5mm) needles; 26 rows and 18 stitches measure 4in (10cm).

70% Shetland wool

30% Merino wool

# Misty morning

**Ingredients:** 1¾oz (50g) of commercially blended combed top of Merino (70%) and soy (30%).

**Method:** Spin equal amounts in the Z direction onto three bobbins using a semi-worsted technique. Ply together in the S direction. The quality of the soft fiber blend results in a warm, cozy yarn.

**Quantity:** Makes 1¾oz (50g) giving around 100yd (90m) finished yarn.

Swatch knitted on US size 7 (4.5mm) needles; 25 rows and 19 stitches measure 4in (10cm).

70% Merino wool

30% soy

# Stormy night

**Ingredients:** ⅞oz (25g) natural gray Shetland wool (1) and ⅞oz (25g) natural black alpaca tops (2).

**Method:** Card together the wool and alpaca and make into rolags. It's not necessary to make a very thorough blend as the different colors add interesting visual texture to the yarn. Spin in the Z direction using a woolen technique onto three separate bobbins. Ply in the S direction for a balanced result.

**Quantity:** Makes 1¾oz (50g), giving around 90yd (80m) finished yarn.

1    2

Swatch knitted on US size 8 (5mm) needles; 24 rows and 14 stitches measure 4in (10cm).

50% Shetland wool

50% alpaca

# Chain-plied color yarn

Swatch knitted on US size 4 (3.5mm) needles; 32 rows and 22 stitches measure 4in (10cm).

CHAIN-PLIED COLOR YARNS ARE DESIGNED TO SHOWCASE COLOR CHANGES BY WORKING WITH FIBERS DYED BEFORE SPINNING.

Using the chain-plying, or Navajo, technique, and managing how frequently the color changes happen, you are in total control over how the colors combine in the final yarn. With rapid changes of color, you can combine different colored plies as you go. Or with longer color sections before changing, you will have sections of three-plied yarns of a single color and, by carefully adjusting the chain length at a color change, you can achieve totally distinct color changes in the finished yarn.

## Applications

Use the chain-ply technique where you want to control color changes in your yarn or to ply a single bobbin or spindle of yarn into a balanced three-ply with no waste.

**Knitting** Multicolored yarns show to good advantage in plain knitting and can give great visual results in two-color knitting techniques such as Fair Isle against a solid color contrast, giving the impression of having used many strands, not just two.

**Weaving** Suitable as both warp and weft yarns, particularly in stripes used as a contrasting highlight.

## Basic recipe: Indian summer

**Cost:** High
**Durability:** High

**Ingredients:** 1¾oz (50g) in total of commercially-dyed rainbow silk top (sections of the top shown here: black [1], purple [2], pink [3], pink/gold transition [4]).

**Quantity:** Makes 1¾oz (50g) giving around 160yd (145m) finished yarn.

1    2    3    4

## Method

**1 Spinning bobbins** Spin all of the fiber onto a single bobbin in the Z direction using a worsted or semi-worsted technique. Spin a generous length of a single color before changing to a different color.

**2 Plying** Use the chain-ply technique (see page 67), plying in the S direction to create a balanced three-ply yarn. Adjust the length of the chain loop at color changes, avoiding overlapping colors.

**3 Finishing** Wind off into a skein, secure with figure-eight ties, wash, and wind into balls when dry.

100% silk

## Top fibers for chain-plied color yarn

• The same fibers as for soft knitting yarn for a soft yarn (see page 82).

• The same fibers as for worsted yarn for a lustrous result (see page 84).

• Commercially prepared rainbow-dyed tops of various fibers, or see page 44 for how to dye your own.

# Spice market

**Cost:** Medium
**Durability:** Medium-high

**Ingredients:** 1¾oz (50g) of commercially-dyed Merino wool tops in a range of colors (shown here: tan [1], green [2], and gold [3]).

**Method:** Spin all of the fiber onto a single bobbin in the Z direction. Spin from the fold (see page 58) and keep changing colors. Ply following the basic method.

**Quantity:** Makes 1¾oz (50g) giving around 120yd (110m) finished yarn.

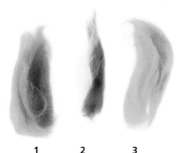

**1      2      3**

Swatch knitted on US size 5 (3.75mm) needles; 32 rows and 23 stitches measure 4in (10cm).

100% Merino wool

# Arabian night

**Cost:** Medium
**Durability:** Medium-high

**Ingredients:** 1¾oz (50g) of natural alpaca, dyed in four colors: orange (1), gold (2), red (3), and green (4).

**Method:** Card each color separately and make into rolags. Spin all the fiber onto one bobbin in the Z direction using a woolen technique changing colors from time to time. Ply following the basic method.

**Quantity:** Makes 1¾oz (50g) giving around 95yd (85m) finished yarn.

**1       2       3       4**

Swatch knitted on US size 5 (3.75mm) needles; 30 rows and 21 stitches measure 4in (10cm).

100% alpaca

# Desert sunset

**Cost:** High
**Durability:** High

**Ingredients:** 1¼oz (35g) dyed tussah silk in pink (1) and gold (2) and ½oz (14g) red mulberry silk top (3).

**Method:** Spin one bobbin in the Z direction using a worsted or semi-worsted method, changing colors as the mood takes you. Remember that your color changes in the final three-ply yarn will be only one-third of the length that you spin as a single. Chain ply the resulting yarn in the S direction, making color shifts by adjusting the size of the chain ply loop where the color changes in the single.

**Quantity:** Makes 1¾oz (50g) giving around 150yd (140m) finished yarn.

**1       2       3**

Swatch knitted on US size 3 (3.25mm) needles; 33 rows and 22 stitches measure 4in (10cm).

70% tussah silk

30% mulberry silk

# Core-spun yarn

CORE-SPUN YARNS ARE COMPLETELY COVERED WITH FIBER. YOUR SELECTION OF CORE YARN AND COVERING FIBERS, COMBINED WITH SUBTLE VARIATIONS IN TECHNIQUE, ALLOWS FOR A WIDE RANGE OF FINISHED YARNS—FROM LOFTY AND AIRY, TO COMPACT AND SMOOTH, TO WILD AND OUTRAGEOUS.

Swatch knitted on US size 10½ (6.5mm) needles; 18 rows and 12 stitches measure 4in (10cm).

Creating a core-spun yarn is a great way of using up a commercially-spun yarn that you find ugly. There is less of a distinction here between the spinning and plying processes, as a core yarn is wholly covered by a layer of pre-drafted fiber or even fabric strips. All manner of found objects can be incorporated. After the first wrapping stage, the yarn may be very out of balance. This can be counteracted by plying with a final fine binder thread, plying in the opposite direction to that of the wrapping, or by adding twist to the core before wrapping.

## Applications

Use core-spun yarn as a main or accent yarn in plain knitting or weaving.

**Knitting** Texture of yarn shows up nicely on both knit and purl sides.

Avoid overly fancy stitch patterns (which can obscure the airy texture).

**Weaving** May be suitable as weft yarns; avoid using in the warp.

## Basic recipe: Tropical twist

**Cost:** Low
**Durability:** Medium

**Ingredients:** 4oz (115g) hand-dyed combed Blue-faced Leicester wool top for the wrapping. At least 95yd (86m) silk or cotton/polyester sewing thread for the core.

**Quantity:** Makes 4oz (115g), giving around 95yd (86m) finished yarn.

99% wool

1% silk or cotton/polyester

## Top fibers for core-spun yarn

• Any hand- or commercially-spun yarn. Since the core is completely covered, this is a good opportunity to use up unsightly, inexpensive, or excess yarn or thread.

• A variety of well-prepared fibers or fabric strips for the wrapping layer. Since wrapping fibers are applied almost perpendicularly to the core, surface shine and texture of a material are really shown off.

• A fine handspun singles or fine commercial yarn for a binder (if used).

• Novelty fibers (slippery nonwools, sparkle, and even found objects), combined with wool for "grip" and wrapped around a core.

## Method

**1 Predrafting** Pre-draft the wrapping fiber. If yo are using a core yarn, run the yarn through the wheel to add twist to it in the same direction as was plied.

**2 Treadling** Attach the core to a leader and star treadle in the opposite direction to the twist of t core yarn.

**3 Plying** Join on wrapping fiber and ply normall for short section to secure.

**4 Wrapping** Pinch the core and wrapping fiber together, then pull the wrapping fiber out to abc a 90-degree angle. Draft the fiber as necessary. Release the pinch, allowing the fiber to wrap the core. Use right-hand distance and tension to gui the wrapping fiber and control the tightness of t wrap. Hold the fiber close to the core to produc denser, more even, and more controlled wrap; h farther away for a looser, airier wrap.

**5 Finishing** Wind off into a skein, wash it to set the twist, and check for balance.

# Woodland walk

**Cost:** Low–medium
**Durability:** Low

**Ingredients:** 40yd (36m) worsted-weight four-ply cotton yarn for core. 2oz (60g) hand-dyed 60/40 wool/hemp top (1) blended with ¾oz (20g) natural light brown Blue-faced leicester/alpaca blend (2) and white 50/50 Merino/Tencel® top for wrapping (3).

**Method:** Follow the basic method, joining the core and wrapper at the beginning, then holding the wrapper fiber out at a 90-degree angle. Hold the fiber-guiding right hand out farther from core, allowing pre-drafted fiber to wrap around more loosely and irregularly for a loftier effect.

**Quantity:** Makes 3½oz (100g), giving around 35yd (32m).

1

2

3

Swatch knitted on US size 13 (9mm) needles; 12 rows and 6 stitches measure 4in (10cm).

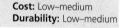

60% wool/hemp

10% Merino/Tencel®

8% cotton

22% wool

# Rainforest green

**Cost:** Low–medium
**Durability:** Low–medium

**Ingredients:** 2¼oz (60g) dyed green Cormo wool roving (1), ½oz (15g) green Romney wool locks (2), ¼oz (7g) dyed pink Merino roving (3), Angelina sparkle (gold iris) for wrapping (4). 60yd (55m) silk or cotton/polyester thread for core.

**Method:** Pre-draft half the green roving. Card the remaining portion with Angelina sparkle and half of the Romney wool locks. Loosen the remaining locks. Tear the pink roving into 2–3in (6–7cm) sections, tying a loose knot in the center of each portion. Follow the basic recipe, joining the core and wrapper at the beginning, then holding the wrapper fiber out at a 90-degree angle. Hold the fiber-guiding right hand close to the core to achieve a denser, closer wrap. Alternate roving blends and add loosened locks (using same wrapping method) and pink roving knots ("flowers"). Non-knotted sections of "flowers" should be held parallel to the core thread and treated as an extension of the core. Continue to wrap green roving around the combined thread/non-knotted portion of the pink roving. As you work up to the knot, allow the wrapping fiber to follow just the core thread, then continue to wrap fiber around the combined thread/non-knotted pink roving below the knot. Due to the "flowers," a large orifice is necessary for this yarn.

**Quantity:** Makes 3oz (85g) giving around 55yd (50m).

1            2

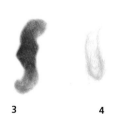

3            4

Swatch knitted on US size 10½ (6.5mm) needles; 16 rows and 10 stitches measure 4in (10 cm).

80% wool

19% carded wool, wool locks, knots, sparkle

1% silk

# Bouclé yarn

BOUCLÉ IS A FRENCH WORD MEANING
"CURLY." THE YARN IS A COMPOUND MIX,
NORMALLY WITH THREE DISTINCT ELEMENTS.

First, bouclé has a strong, smooth, and fine core
yarn; silk is ideal for this. Next is the main
wrapper—this is the one that bunches up or loops;
mohair is perfect due to its characteristic corkscrew
twist. The final element is a fine-yarn binder,
stabilizing the yarn and balancing the twist.

Swatch knitted on US size 10 (6 mm) needles; 20 rows
and 15 stitches measure 4 in. (10 cm).

## Applications

Use bouclé yarn as an accent yarn in plain
knitting or weaving.

**Knitting** Texture of yarn will show up better on
the purl side. Avoid fancy stitch patterns (which
will not show up well).

**Weaving** Avoid using in the warp—it may be
problematic passing through the heddles or
the reed.

## Basic recipe:
## Crème fraîche

**Cost:** Medium
**Durability:** Low

**Ingredients:** For each of core and
binder, 88yd (80m) commercially-
spun 60/2 ecru silk (1); for the
wrapper, 1½ oz (45g) natural
wool roving (2).

**Quantity:** Makes 1¾oz (50g) giving
around 88yd (80m) finished yarn.

85%
wool

15%
silk

1            2

## Top fibers for bouclé yarn

• For the core yarn, silk is ideal: either
a commercial yarn or finely and firmly
handspun; other smooth, fine yarns
can also be used.

• For the wrapper, mohair is
particularly suitable because of the
way it curls, but many other fibers
can be used with good results, for
example wool and cotton.

• The binder may be the same fiber
or commercial yarn as the core, but
provided it is finer than the wrapper,
other fibers or yarns may be used.

## Method

**1 Spinning** If not using a commercially-plied core, spin the
core yarn in the S direction. Use the worsted technique
(see pages 54–55) and give it plenty of twist; although fine
it needs to be fairly robust. Spin the wrapper yarn in the
normal Z direction. If applicable, spin the fine binder yarn
in the S direction.

**2 Plying** Prepare to ply the core and the wrapper in the
S direction. Hold the core yarn under firm tension but
apply very light tension to the wrapper yarn and let it
wrap gently round the core.

**3 Wrapping** After wrapping about 4in (10cm), begin to
push up the curls (see page 71). Repeat the plying and
pushing actions. You are aiming for a plied yarn that has
some S-twist remaining, not a balanced yarn at this stage.

**4 Binding** Ply the two-ply yarn and the binder yarn in the
Z direction to secure the curls and balance the yarn.

**5 Finishing** Wind off into a skein, wash it to set the twist,
and check for balance.

# Chili dip

**Cost:** Medium–high
**Durability:** Low

**Ingredients:** Core: ¼oz (5g) dark red silk roving (1). Wrapper: 1½oz (45g) dark red Merino wool top (2). Binder: ¼oz (5g) natural brown alpaca (3).

**Method:** Follow the standard method, plying the wrapper round the core in the S direction and then plying with the binder in the Z direction.

**Quantity:** Makes about 1¾oz (50g) giving around 80yd (72m) finished yarn.

1    2    3

Swatch knitted on US size 9 (5.5mm) needles; 20 rows and 14 stitches measure 4in (10cm).

15% silk

70% Merino

15% alpaca

# Lemon curd

**Cost:** Medium–high
**Durability:** Low

**Ingredients:** Core: ¼oz (5g) pre-drafted natural tussah silk brick (1). Wrapper: 1½oz (45g) prepared yellow kid mohair (2). Binder: ¼oz (5g) of the same silk brick as the core (1).

**Method:** Follow the basic recipe method, plying the wrapper round the core in S direction and then plying with the binder in the Z direction.

**Quantity:** Makes 1¾oz (50g), giving around 75yd (68m) finished yarn.

1    2

Swatch knitted on US size 7 (4.5mm) needles; 24 rows and 16 stitches measure 4in (10cm).

15% silk

85% mohair

# Butterfly blue

**Cost:** Medium–high
**Durability:** Low

**Ingredients:** Core: about 82yd (75m) lilac polyester sewing thread (1). Wrapper: 1½oz (45g) blue kid mohair (2) blended with ¼oz (5g) tri-lobal nylon (3). Binder: 82yd (75m) green metallic sewing thread (4).

**Method:** Follow the basic recipe method, plying the wrapper round the core in the S direction and then plying with the binder in the Z direction.

**Quantity:** Makes 1¾oz (50g), giving 82yd (75m) finished yarn.

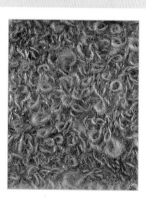

1    2

3    4

Swatch knitted on US size 6 (4mm) needles; 26 rows and 18 stitches measure 4in (10cm).

2% polyester sewing thread

10% nylon

85% mohair

3% metallic sewing

# Paper yarn

THESE PAPER YARNS ARE DESIGNED MAINLY FOR ART AND CRAFT USES AND TO GIVE YOU THE CHALLENGE—AND PURE JOY—OF SPINNING UNCONVENTIONAL MATERIALS.

Experienced spinners could experiment with different papers for these yarns—this is not recommended for beginners. Think about flexibility and durability if you are planning a practical end use. The paper is cut into long, thin strips before twist is added to create a yarn, so there is no drafting involved. The strips are often cut almost from edge to edge of a sheet, so you will need to manage the little bumps at the turn of the cuts. Any joins need to be long overlapped tapers, so that plenty of twist can hold the join together. The yarn may be plied in the usual way.

## Basic recipe: Ticker-tape yellow

**Cost:** Low
**Durability:** Low

**Ingredients:** One packet of crepe paper cut into ⅜in (1cm) strips.

**Quantity:** Makes 1¾oz (50g) giving around 88yd (80m) finished yarn.

100%
crepe paper

## Applications

Use paper yarns where textural interest would be an advantage, and durability is not an issue, especially in craft projects.

**Knitting** Not normally suitable.

**Weaving** May be suitable as weft yarns.

**Other** Baskets, tassels.

## Top paper for paper yarn

- Crepe paper (fairly resilient but with some flexibility).

- Tissue paper (for fineness).

- Greaseproof paper or baking parchment (for crisp texture).

## Method

**1 Spinning bobbins** Spin two equal bobbins in the Z direction, taking care that the spun "yarn" does not catch around the hooks of the flyer.

**2 Plying** Ply together normally in the S direction until balanced.

**3 Finishing** Wind off into a skein, secure with figure-eight ties, and wind loosely into balls.

# Manilla

**Ingredients:** About 1.5sq yd (1.25 sq m) baking parchment.

**Method:** Cut the paper sheets across in ¾in (2cm) strips but stop the cut short of the edge of the paper. Turn the sheet around and cut down the middle of those strips, stopping short of the edge. This gives you a long zig-zag strip. Carefully spin in the Z direction, rolling the lumps that result at the edge turns. Taper and overlap the strips and guide the twist into the join. Spin two bobbins in this way and ply together in the S direction.

**Quantity:** Makes 1¾oz (50g) giving around 50yd (45m) finished yarn.

100% baking parchment paper

# Envelope white

**Ingredients:** About 25 sheets of absorbent industrial-strength paper towel.

**Method:** Follow the method for "Manilla," cutting across the width of the paper roll and stopping short of the edges. The wider and stronger paper will make spinning easier, but beware of the possibility of paper cuts to your fingers as you spin.

**Quantity:** Makes 1¾oz (50g) giving around 66yd (60m) finished yarn.

100% paper towel

# Post-it pink

**Ingredients:** About 12 sheets colored tissue paper.

**Method:** Follow the method for "Manilla," cutting across the width of the sheets and stopping short of the edges. Tissue paper spins quite well into a yarn with reasonable flexibility and less risk of paper cuts. The dyes in colored tissue paper may run when wet, so take this into account when planning a project.

**Quantity:** Makes 1¾oz (50g) giving around 45yd (40m) finished yarn.

100% tissue paper

# Bullion yarn

BULLION YARNS ARE DESIGNED TO HAVE VISUAL INTEREST WITH A STRONGLY TEXTURED CHARACTER. THE "BULLIONS" ARE BUILT UP BY ALLOWING ONE OF THE PLIES TO WRAP AROUND THE OTHER IN A CONCENTRATED AREA.

Swatch knitted on US size 6 (4mm) needles; 30 rows and 20 stitches measure 4in (10cm).

A bullion yarn can be thought of as a further development of the spiral yarn technique. As in a spiral yarn, one of the plies wraps loosely around the other, but here in concentrated zones. The resulting bullions are separated by sections of evenly tensioned conventional two-ply yarn. Color differences between the two plies can be used to great effect so that the bullions contrast with the background, and by switching the roles of the two single elements, the color of the bullions can be exchanged. If the core is slippery, a final wrapper ply may be necessary to keep the bullions from sliding along the yarn—see "Lavender," opposite.

## Applications

Use bullion yarns where textural interest would be an advantage.

**Knitting** Use with plain stitches. The texture of the yarn will be predominant on the purl rather than the knit side of the fabric.

**Weaving** Suitable as weft yarns, especially as an accent against a ground of a smooth yarn. The texture may be problematic in the warp due to abrasion in the reed.

## Basic recipe: Iris

**Cost:** Medium
**Durability:** Medium–low

**Ingredients:** ⅞oz (25g) colored Merino top (1) and ⅞oz (25g) of blended wool and mohair. The wool used here was a top of Blue-faced Leicester (BFL) (2) and the mohair was a blue-dyed top (3).

**Quantity:** Makes 1¾oz (50g), giving around 88yd (80m) finished yarn.

1   2   3

| | |
|---|---|
| 50% Merino wool | |
| 30% BFL wool | |
| 20% mohair | |

## Top fibers for bullion yarn

• The best fibers for bullion yarns are the same fibers as for lustrous worsted yarns (see page 84).

• Rainbow-dyed fibers work as a contrast to a solid-colored base and enable you to make different-colored bullions.

## Method

**1 Preparation** Prepare and spin each color separately in the Z direction, using a worsted or semi-worsted technique (see page 54).

**2 Plying** Prepare to ply in the S direction, holding both plies under firm tension, and ply normally for a short distance.

**3 Forming bullions** Working close to the orifice, relax the tension on one ply, move your hand out to the side, and guide it backward and forward to wrap the taut strand and form a bullion. If you wish, exchange the role of the plies from time to time, aiming for a balanced result. See page 73 for more on the bullion technique.

**4 Finishing** Wind off into a skein, secure with figure-eight ties, wash, and wind into balls when dry.

# Hyacinth

**Cost:** Medium
**Durability:** Medium–low

**Ingredients:** ⅞oz (25g) blue mohair top (1) and ⅞oz (25g) carded linen/silk fiber blend.

**Method:** Spin the mohair in the Z direction using a worsted technique. On a separate bobbin, spin the linen/silk blend in the Z direction using a woolen technique. Follow the basic method for plying and forming bullions (see opposite).

**Quantity:** Makes 1¾oz (50g), giving around 135yd (125m) finished yarn.

1          2

Swatch knitted on US size 4 (3.5mm) needles; 28 rows and 20 stitches measure 4in (10cm).

50% mohair

30% linen

20% silk

# Lavender

**Cost:** High
**Durability:** Medium

**Ingredients:** 1000yd (900m) blue commercially-spun 2/60s silk (1); ½oz (14g) rainbow-dyed mawata silk (2).

**Method:** Separate the single layers of the mawata, break a hole in the middle, and draft into a fine roving. Spin in the Z direction using a worsted technique. On a separate bobbin, spin together in the Z direction three strands of 2/60s silk 250yd (225m) long. Follow the standard method for plying in the S direction and making bullions, using the mawata silk for bullions and the 2/60s silk as the core, adding extra

plying twist. Ply once more in the Z direction, using a strand of 2/60s silk as a wrapper.

**Quantity:** Makes 1¾oz (50g) giving around 220yd (200m) finished yarn.

1          2

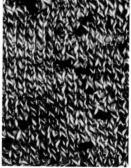

Swatch knitted on US size 5 (3.75mm) needles; 32 rows and 22 stitches measure 4in (10cm).

70% 2/60s commercial silk yarn

30% mawata silk

# Foxglove

**Cost:** Medium–low
**Durability:** Medium

**Ingredients:** ¾oz (20g) natural ramie (1) and 1oz (30g) Merino tops (2–4), in shades of purple.

**Method:** Spin the ramie and the Merino onto separate bobbins in the Z direction using a worsted or semi-worsted technique. Ply in the S direction and create the bullions following the basic recipe method, using the ramie as the core and the Merino to make the bullions.

**Quantity:** Makes 1¾oz (50g) giving around 160yd (145m) finished yarn.

1      2      3      4

Swatch knitted on US size 5 (3.75mm) needles; 36 rows and 24 stitches measure 4in (10cm).

60% Merino wool

40% ramie

# Chapter 4

# Projects

*This chapter illustrates some ideas for incorporating your own handspun yarn into unique projects, including techniques for knitting, weaving, and tassel making. The projects aim to show you how to adapt the patterns to yarn of any given size and to inspire you to create individual and well-fitting items.*

# Woven pillow cover

IF YOU ARE A WEAVER, YOU CAN GAIN CONFIDENCE WEAVING WITH HANDSPUN IF YOU FIRST USE IT IN THE WEFT, WHERE YOU CAN USE A SINGLES YARN—YOU DON'T ALWAYS HAVE TO PLY. THIS WOVEN DESIGN IS BASED ON UNDULATING TWILL ON A BASIC FOUR-SHAFT LOOM. THE ORIGAMI-LIKE CONSTRUCTION IS A NEAT WAY TO MAKE A SQUARE 40 PERCENT WIDER THAN YOUR WOVEN FABRIC.

## Figuring size and quantities

For a square pillow, decide on the finished size of the pillow. The following assumes that you will achieve a balanced weave (the same number of warp ends and weft picks per inch [or per cm]), so is an approximation. Check that you have enough yarn (see page 132) before proceeding.

**Warp** First, figure the width in the reed of the warp. Take the width of the pillow, add on at least 10 percent allowance for takeup and shrinkage and divide this

## >> Equipment

- A four-shaft loom, shuttle, and standard weaving accessories, enabling you to wind a warp, thread the loom, and weave
- Tapestry needle
- Pins, needles, and thread
- Sewing machine (optional)
- Pillow form or batting

## >> Yarns

The hand-spun singles yarn is a worsted-spun silk and cashmere blend, and the twist was set using a steam iron. The commercial warp yarn is a two-ply superwash Merino. The warp and weft yarns should be of a similar size. Figure the sett as two-thirds of the wraps per inch. You will also need a square pillow form or batting.

## >> Project details

**Pillow size:** 13½ x 13½in (30 x 30cm) for a 12 x 12in (30 x 30cm) pillow pad

**Yarn one:** slate brown handspun (weft)
**Fiber:** worsted-spun silk/cashmere blend
**Spun as:** unplied singles yarn; set using a steam iron
**Wraps per inch:** 27 (11 wpc)
**Yards per pound:** 2500yd/lb (5000m/kg)
**Quantity for project:** 250yd; 1½oz (225m; 45g)

**Yarn two:** white commercial (warp)
**Fiber:** 100% superwash Merino wool
**Spun as:** worsted type two-ply
**Wraps per inch:** 27 (11 wpc)
**Yards per pound:** 7000yd/lb (14000m/kg)
**Sett:** 18 ends per inch (7 epc)
**Width in reed:** 10in (25cm)
**Number of ends:** 180
**Quantity for project:** 360yd; ⅞oz (330m; 25g)

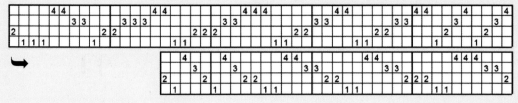

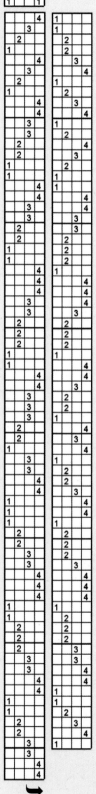

number by a factor of 1.4. The result is the width of the warp in the reed.

Next, figure the number of warp ends you will need. Multiply the width of the warp in inches by the number of ends per inch or sett. The sett should be about two-thirds of the wraps per inch.

Figure the length of the warp you will need to wind. Take the width of fabric to be woven, multiply by four and add two seam allowances. Add to this an allowance for take-up and shrinkage of at least 10 percent. This is the main warp length. Finally, add on an appropriate allowance for front and back loom waste (according to your own loom) and for sampling. This is the total warp length.

Total warp yarn required is number of warp ends x total warp length.

**Weft** The approximate total weft yarn required equals main warp length multiplied by number of warp ends.

## Weaving

Wind the warp, and dress and thread the loom according to the threading plan and weave according to the treadling plan (see above and right). The size of the pattern repeats can be adjusted to suit the width of your weaving. It is very desirable to weave and wet-finish a sample before completing the main piece. Weave a

length of fabric about four and a half times its width. Remove from the loom and stabilize the ends to keep them from raveling, before wet-finishing. After shrinkage, you should have a piece more than four times the pillow's length, leaving an allowance for seams.

## Making up

This is easier to do than describe in words, and I recommend you practice by folding a paper strip first.

Referring to the diagrams below, mark the midpoint, E, then with right sides together, seam the ends AB to CD so that you have a wide tube. Press the seam open then turn the tube so that the seam is on the inside with the wrong sides now together.

Align the seam and the marked point E and pin the tube flat. Hand-sew one pair of selvages together in this position using a flat seam (hand sew the selvages edge to edge without taking up any seam allowance). Remove the pins and open out the pillow with the hand-sewn seam forming a diagonal of the square.

Turn the pillow over and pin the square so that the remaining selvages lie together. Press flat.

Insert the pillow form or batting and hand sew the remaining selvages in a flat seam.

Above: The threading plan. Add a floating selvage at each side. Right and above right: The treadling plan and tie-up.

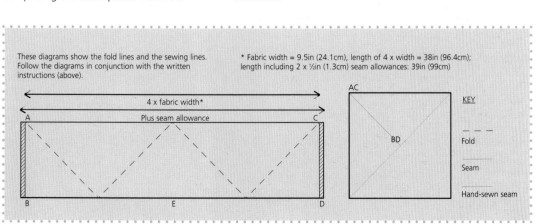

These diagrams show the fold lines and the sewing lines. Follow the diagrams in conjunction with the written instructions (above).

* Fabric width = 9.5in (24.1cm), length of 4 x width = 38in (96.4cm); length including 2 x ½in (1.3cm) seam allowances: 39in (99cm)

4 x fabric width*

Plus seam allowance

A · · · · · · · · · · · · · · · · · · · · · · · · C

B · · · · · · · · · · · E · · · · · · · · · · · D

AC

BD

KEY

- - - -  Fold

———  Seam

———  Hand-sewn seam

# Knitted hat and mittens

THIS HAT AND MITTENS, BOTH WORKED IN THE ROUND ON DOUBLE-POINTED OR CIRCULAR NEEDLES, ARE MADE OF A LOVELY, NATURAL ALPACA/SILK BLEND. THEY ARE EXTREMELY COZY AND FIT PERFECTLY. THE ACCENT OF JUST A FEW ROWS OF CONTRASTING KID MOHAIR YARN GIVE A HARMONIOUS FEEL TO THE SET AND ENABLES A SMALL AMOUNT OF THE FEATURE YARN TO STAND OUT BEAUTIFULLY. FOR A LOVELY SOFT EDGE TO THE RIBBING, USE A CAST-ON WITH SOME STRETCH. A TUBULAR CAST-ON WAS USED HERE.

## Preparation

Cast on 20 or more stitches using what you guess to be an appropriate needle size and work several rows in stockinette stitch, changing needle size if necessary to get the right feel—a smaller size for a closer-fitting result or a larger size if the swatch feels too solid. Make a note of how many stitches and rows you get to the inch (2.5cm).

Make a separate test swatch of a few rows in k1 p1 rib using a slightly smaller needle size for an appropriate handle to the rib sample. Measure how many stitches you get to the inch when the sample is fully stretched, slightly stretched, and relaxed.

Figure approximately how much yarn you will need in total (see page 132) to ensure you have enough before proceeding with the main items. As a rough guide, see the project specifications on pages 114 and 115.

## Making the mittens

Start by translating all the measurements on the diagram on page 114 into stitches or rows and then refer to these calculations at each stage of the knitting so that the mitten will fit perfectly with some ease for movement. The cuff should sit fairly snugly around the wrist, but it's essential that it stretches sufficiently to allow the mittens on and off! Calculate the number of relaxed or very slightly stretched stitches that equate to the wrist circumference. Next, figure out the number of fully stretched stitches needed for the widest part of the hand, measured around the base of the thumb. Take the higher of these two stitch numbers, rounded up to an even number. For these mittens, that number was 32 stitches on US size 4 (3.5mm) needles for the ribbed cuff, and US size 6 (4mm) for the stockinette stitch main body. Follow the general method on pages 114–115 and adjust the number of stitches and rows if necessary for your yarn and hand measurements.

## Making the hat

Measure the circumference of your head, and figure out how many stretched rib stitches you need. Choose an even number appropriate to your yarn, head size, and needles. Follow the pattern on pages 115–116.

*continued* ▶

### >> Equipment

● Circular or double-pointed knitting needles (approx. US sizes 4 and 6 [3.5mm and 4mm])
● Tape measure
● Two safety pins
● Cable needle
● Pom-pom maker or cardboard disks (optional)

### >> Yarns

The main yarn is spun semi-worsted (from the fold) as a balanced two-ply from a commercial blend of natural gray alpaca and ecru silk. The contrast yarn is spun woolen (long-draw from rolags) as a balanced two-ply from rainbow-dyed kid mohair. This yarn blooms beautifully on washing and the halo will develop further with use. Both yarns are spun to a similar thickness.

### >> Abbreviations

For a full list of knitting abbreviations, see page 116.

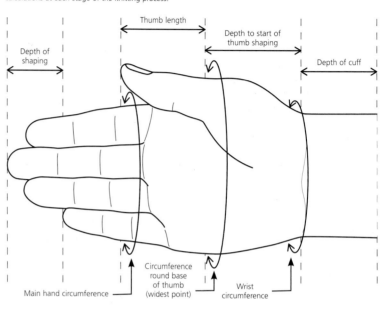

Calculate the below measurements (on your own hand) and make a note. Then translate them into stitches or rows and refer to these calculations at each stage of the knitting process.

## >> Mitten project details

**Size:** main hand circumference 7in (18cm); length 10½in (27cm)
**Gauge:** 23 stitches and 26 rows to 4in (10cm) worked in stockinette stitch

**Yarn one (MC):** gray handspun
**Fiber:** commercial blend of natural gray alpaca and ecru silk
**Spun as:** semi-worsted (from the fold) as a balanced two-ply
**Wraps per inch:** 12 (4.7 wpc)
**Yards per pound:** 1000yd/lb (2000m/kg)
**Quantity of MC yarn:** about 120yd (110m); 2oz (55g)

**Yarn two (CC):** rainbow-dyed handspun
**Fiber:** kid mohair
**Spun as:** woolen (long-draw from rolags) as a balanced two-ply
**Wraps per inch:** 12 (4.7 wpc)
**Yards per pound:** 2000yd/lb (4000 m/kg)
**Quantity of CC yarn:** 10yd (9m); ⅛oz (5g)

## Knitting patterns

### Right mitten

With MC and your preferred cast-on method, cast on 32 stitches or the number required for the cuff, with a circular needle or a set of double-pointed needles, US size 4 (3.5mm).

**Work cuff**
Rounds 1–14: [K1, p1] to the end of the round. (If you adjust for a different depth of cuff, keep careful count of the number of rounds knitted and keep a written record so that you can work the second mitten to match.)

**Work main body of mitten**
Change needles to US size 6 (4mm).
Rounds 15–18: Knit.

**Work contrast bands as folls**
Round 19: With CC, knit.
Round 20: With CC, purl.
Round 21: With MC, knit.
Rounds 22–24: Repeat rounds 19–21.
Cont using MC and start shaping for base of thumb.
Round 25: Kfb, k to end of round

(33 sts).
Round 26: Knit.
Rounds 27–40: Repeat rounds 25–26 (40 sts).

**Divide for thumb**
Round 41: Slip next 7 sts onto a safety pin and cast on 6 replacement sts, k to end of round (39 sts).
Round 42: K into front and back [Kfb] of each of the first 6 sts, kspto end of round (45 sts).
Round 43: [K1, sl1 onto cable needle at front] 6 times, slip the 6 sts on the cable needle onto a second safety pin and k to end of round (39 sts). If using double-pointed needles, redistribute the stitches evenly between the needles.

**Continue main body**
Rounds 44–64: Knit.

**Work contrast band**
Rounds 65–66: With CC, repeat rounds 19–20.

**Continue, using MC, with the body**
Rounds 67–70: With MC, knit. Begin shaping top of mitten—paired decreases and single decreases give an asymmetrical shape in accordance with the shape of the hand.
Round 71: K2tog, k16, sl1 k1 psso, k2tog, k16, sl1 (36 sts).
Round 72: K1, psso, k15, sl1 k1 psso, k2tog, k15 (33 sts).
Round 73: K2tog, k13, sl1 k1 psso, k2tog, k13, sl1 (30 sts).
Round 74: K1, psso, k12, sl1 k1 psso, k2tog, k12 (27 sts).
Round 75: K2tog, k10, sl1 k1 psso, k2tog, k10, sl1 (24 sts).
Round 76: K1, psso, k9, sl1 k1 psso, k2tog, k9 (21 sts).
Round 77: K2tog, k7, sl1 k1 psso, k2tog, k7, sl1 (18 sts).
Round 78: K1, psso, k6, sl1 k1 psso, k2tog, k6 (15 sts).
Round 79: K2tog, k to end (14 sts). Join the top of the mitten using Kitchener stitch (grafting).

**Work thumb**
Arrange the 13 reserved sts onto 3 double-pointed needles, and with MC, knit 13 rounds or until the desired thumb depth is worked. Shape top of thumb.
Next round: [Sl1, k2tog, psso] twice, k1, [sl1, k2tog, psso] twice (5 sts).
Join the top of the thumb using Kitchener stitch (grafting).

## Left mitten
Work first 24 rounds as for right mitten. Resume in MC and start shaping for base of thumb.
Round 25: K to end of round, M1.
Round 26: Knit.
Rounds 27–40: Repeat rounds 25–26 (40 sts).

**Divide for thumb**
Round 41: K to last 7 sts, slip them onto a safety pin and cast on 6 replacement sts (39 sts).

Round 42: K to last 6 sts, [kfb] 6 times (45 sts).
Round 43: K to last 12 sts, [K1, sl1 onto cable needle at front] 6 times and slip the 6 sts on the cable needle onto a second safety pin (39 sts). If using double-pointed needles, redistribute the stitches evenly between the needles.
Round 44 onward and thumb: As for right mitten.

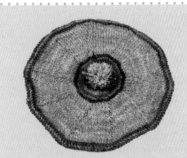

## >> Hat project details

**Size:** head circumference 22–23in (56–58cm); diameter 11½in (29cm)
**Gauge:** 23 stitches and 26 rows to 4in (10cm) worked in stockinette stitch

**Yarn one (MC):** gray handspun
**Fiber:** commercial blend of natural gray alpaca and ecru silk
**Spun as:** semi-worsted (from the fold) as a balanced two-ply
**Wraps per inch:** 12 (4.7 wpc)
**Yards per pound:** 1000yd/lb (2000m/kg)
**Quantity of MC yarn:** about 150yd (140m); 2½oz (70g)

**Yarn two (CC):** rainbow-dyed handspun
**Fiber:** kid mohair
**Spun as:** woolen (long-draw from rolags) as a balanced two-ply
**Wraps per inch:** 12 (4.7 wpc)
**Yards per pound:** 2000yd/lb (4000m/kg)
**Quantity of CC yarn:** 10yd (9m); ⅛ oz (5g)

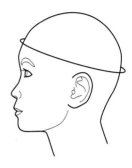

Measure your own head circumference and translate that measurement into the number of stitches (stretched) for the rib.

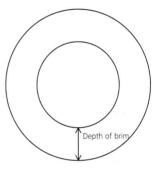

Head circumference equates to circumference of stretched rib

Depth of brim

## Hat
With MC and your preferred cast-on method, cast on 102 stitches or the number required for the rib, with a circular needle or a set of double-pointed needles, US size 4 (3.5mm).

**Work rib**
Rounds 1–10: [K1, p1] to the end of the round.

**Work underside of brim**
Change to US size 6 (4mm) needles.
Round 11: Knit.
Round 12: K1, [kfb, k19] 4 times, kfb, k20 (107 sts).
Round 13: K7, [kfb, k20] 4 times, kfb, k15 (112 sts).
Round 14: K14, [kfb, k21] 4 times, kfb, k9 (117 sts).
Round 15: K1, [kfb, k22] 4 times, kfb, k23 (122 sts).
Round 16: K7, [kfb, k23] 4 times, kfb, k18 (127 sts).

continued ▶

◀ *continued from previous page*

**Round 17:** K14, [kfb, k24] 4 times, kfb, k12 (132 sts).
**Round 18:** K1, [kfb, k25] 4 times, kfb, k26 (137 sts).
**Round 19:** K7, [kfb, k26] 4 times, kfb, k21 (142 sts).
**Round 20:** K14, [kfb, k27] 4 times, kfb, k15 (147 sts).
**Round 21:** K1, [kfb, k28] 4 times, kfb, k29 (152 sts).
**Round 22:** K7, [kfb, k59] 2 times, kfb, k24 (155 sts).

**Work contrast bands**
**Round 23:** With CC, knit.
**Round 24:** With CC, purl.
**Round 25:** With MC, knit.
**Rounds 26–28:** Repeat rounds 23–25.

**Work top of hat**
**Round 29:** [K29, k2tog] 5 times (150 sts).
**Round 30:** K14, k2tog, [k28, k2tog] 4 times, k14 (145 sts).
**Round 31:** [K27, k2tog] 5 times (140 sts).
**Round 32:** K13, k2tog, [k26, k2tog] 4 times, k13 (135 sts).
**Round 33:** [K25, k2tog] 5 times (130 sts).
**Round 34:** K12, k2tog, [k24, k2tog] 4 times, k12 (125 sts).
**Round 35:** [K23, k2tog] 5 times (120 sts).
**Round 36:** K11, k2tog, [k22, k2tog] 4 times, k11 (115 sts).
**Round 37:** [K21, k2tog] 5 times (110 sts).
**Round 38**: K10, k2tog, [k20, k2tog] 4 times, k10 (105 sts).
**Round 39:** [K19, k2tog] 5 times (100 sts).
**Round 40:** K9, k2tog, [k18, k2tog] 4 times, k9 (95 sts).
**Round 41:** [K17, k2tog] 5 times (90 sts).
**Round 42:** K8, k2tog, [k16, k2tog] 4 times, k8 (85 sts).
**Round 43:** [K15, k2tog] 5 times (80 sts).
**Round 44:** K7, k2tog, [k14, k2tog] 4 times, k7 (75 sts).
**Round 45:** [K13, k2tog] 5 times (70 sts).
**Round 46:** K6, k2tog, [k12, k2tog] 4 times, k6 (65 sts).

**Work contrast bands**
**Round 47:** With CC, [k11, k2tog] 5 times (60 sts).
**Round 48:** With CC, p5, p2tog, [p10, p2tog] 4 times, p5 (55 sts).
**Round 49:** With MC, [k9, k2tog] 5 times (50 sts).
**Round 50:** With CC, k4, k2tog, [k8, k2tog] 4 times, k4 (45 sts).
**Round 51:** With CC, purl.

**Continue, using MC, with top of hat**
**Round 52:** [K7, k2tog] 5 times (40 sts).
**Round 53:** K3, k2tog, [k6, k2tog] 4 times, k3 (35 sts).
**Round 54:** [K5, k2tog] 5 times (30 sts).
**Round 55:** K2, k2tog, [k4, k2tog] 4 times , k2 (25 sts).
**Round 56:** [K3, k2tog] 5 times (20 sts).
**Round 57:** K1, k2tog, [k2, k2tog] 4 times, k1 (15 sts).
**Round 58:** [K1, k2tog] 5 times (10 sts).
**Round 59:** [K2tog] 5 times (5 sts).
**Round 60:** [K2tog] twice, k1 (3 sts).
Bind off.

**Finishing**
Add pom-poms to your taste (see panel below). Weave in the ends and block the items lightly. The hat could be blocked over a 10in (25cm) dinner plate.

---

**ABBREVIATIONS**
**K:** knit
**P:** purl
**Kfb:** knit into the front and back of the stitch
**M1:** lift the strand between the last stitch and the next stitch and knit into the back of it
**K2tog:** knit two stitches together
**psso:** pass the slipped stitch over
**sl1:** slip the stitch from the left to the right needle, as if to knit it, but without doing so
**MC:** main color
**CC:** contrast color
**cont:** continue
**folls:** follows
**[ ]:** repeat the instruction inside the brackets as specified after the brackets

---

**>> Try this next**

A pom-pom maker is a great time-saving tool if you have a number of pom-poms to make, but for just one, you can use a homemade cardboard form. Cut two equal disks the same diameter as the pom-pom you wish to make, and cut large matching central holes in each. Hold the two rings together and wind the yarn around and around the edge of the ring until the central hole is fairly full. With sharp scissors, carefully cut the yarn at the outer edges of the rings, pressing the points of the scissors between the two rings. Separate the rings slightly and make a very firm tie around the center with a doubled length of yarn. Finally, pull the rings away, fluff up the pom-pom, and make any final trimming adjustments. Use the tails of the center tie to attach the pom-pom to the center of the hat.

# Tassels

THESE EXUBERANT TASSELS USE SPUN PAPER FOR THE MAIN SKIRT, WHICH GIVES A RUSTLING SOUND WHEN SHAKEN. THEY ARE EASY TO MAKE AND ENABLE YOU TO SHOWCASE UNUSUAL YARNS TO GREAT EFFECT. USE FOR TIE-BACKS OR HANG ON AN INTERNAL DOOR KNOB AS A DESIGN FEATURE.

## Cover the mold

Cover a section of the tassel mold with adhesive and carefully stick the yarn around the mold under tension, neatly winding over the starting end. Continue to ▶

### >> Equipment

- Tassel mold
- PVA adhesive and small brush or glue gun
- Craft wire
- Tassel skirt board or very stout piece of cardboard
- Medium-sized knitting needle
- One ¾in (1.9cm) wooden disk

### >> Yarns

Almost any yarn can be used in a tassel, from the most luxurious silk for a skirt with beautiful drape, to roughly spun jute for a tassel to adorn a garden shed. In these examples, the main yarn in the skirt of each tassel is a two-ply spun from crepe paper. The yarns covering the mold and in the suspension cord of tassel 1 are natural white ramie and dark purple tussah silk. The silk also forms mini tassels on the skirt. Both the ramie and silk are two-ply worsted-spun yarns. Tassel 2 has an underskirt of natural cream soy silk and both yarns are used to cover the tassel mold and to make the suspension cord.

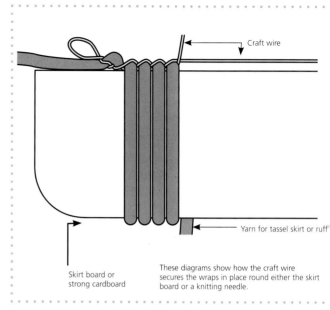

Craft wire

Yarn for tassel skirt or ruff

Skirt board or strong cardboard

These diagrams show how the craft wire secures the wraps in place round either the skirt board or a knitting needle.

## << Project details: tassel 1

**Tassel height from the top of the head to the bottom of the underskirt:**
8in (20cm)
**Tassel mold:** 2.5in (6.4cm) diameter double-round head

**Yarn one:** white handspun
**Fiber:** spun crepe paper
**Spun as:** two-ply
**Wraps per inch:** 11 (4.3 wpc)
**Yards per pound:** 800yd/lb (1600m/kg)
**Quantity for a 4in (10cm) skirt:** 225yd (205m)

**Yarn two:** off-white handspun
**Fiber:** ramie
**Spun as:** worsted-spun two-ply
**Wraps per inch:** 20 (8 wpc)
**Yards per pound:** 1500yd/lb (3000m/kg)
**Quantity for the suspension cord and to cover mold:** 10yd (9m)

**Yarn three:** purple handspun
**Fiber:** tussah silk
**Ply:** worsted-spun two-ply
**Wraps per inch:** 30 (12 wpc)
**Yards per pound:** 2000yd/lb (4000m/kg)
**Quantity for the suspension cord to cover mold and ruff:** 30yd (27m)

apply adhesive to each successive section (so that it doesn't dry out before you have finished) and completely cover the outside of the mold, changing yarns as you go.

## Make and fit the skirt

Take a piece of craft wire about four times the circumference of the tassel, fold it in half, and twist a small loop in the end. Lay one end of the wire along the top edge of the skirt board or stout cardboard, leaving the other wire pointing upward. Wind the skirt yarn around the board over the first wire. Give the two wires a single twist so that they change places and secure the skirt yarn in place. Continue in the same way to complete the skirt, sliding the work along the board until you have enough to fit around the mold.

Fit the skirt around the mold and secure by passing the end wires through the starting small loop. Twist and trim the excess. Bury the ends beneath the skirt.

A tassel ruff can be made in the same way, but using a knitting needle instead of a skirt board as the template. Work away from the point of the needle toward the knob so that you can slide the completed part off the point as you work if you need more length.

## Make and attach a suspension cord

A suspension cord is quite chunky, so take several ends of the yarn you wish to use

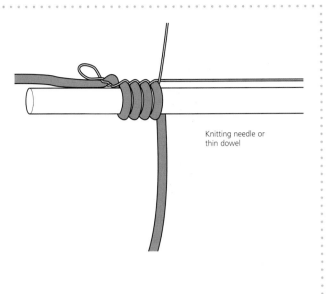

Knitting needle or
thin dowel

and add extra twist in the same direction.
A hand spindle is ideal, because you will
be dealing with a short length. Allow the
twisted yarns to self-ply until balanced.
Pass the loop through the central hole in
the mold and skirt through the wooden
disk to secure.

## Finishing touches
Make a soft tassel by simply winding a
quantity of yarn around a mold, such as
a piece of strong cardboard or a book of
an appropriate size, and tying through
the loops in the center to secure. Cut
through opposite the center, fold in half,
and bind around to finish. Tassel 1, left,
shows supplementary mini tassels
attached over the main skirt. Alternatively,
make the tassel longer than the overskirt
to show below, and attached to the base
of the mold, within the overskirt (see
tassel 2, right, where the underskirt also
has a tie midway).

## >> Project details: tassel 2

**Tassel height from the top of the head
to the bottom of the underskirt:**
10in (25cm)
**Tassel mold:** 3in (7.6cm) diameter
tapering head

**Yarn one:** black handspun
**Fiber:** spun crepe paper
**Spun as:** two-ply
**Wraps per inch:** 12 (4.7 wpc)
**Yards per pound:** 800yd/lb
(1600m/kg)
**Quantity for the suspension cord to
cover mold and 2¾in (7cm) skirt:**
150yd (137m)

**Yarn two:** cream handspun
**Fiber:** soy silk
**Spun as:** worsted-spun two-ply
**Wraps per inch:** 20 (8 wpc)
**Yards per pound:** 1800yd/lb
(3600m/kg)
**Quantity for the suspension cord to
cover mold, 4in (10cm) skirt, and ruff:**
55yd (50m)

# Knitted slipcase

THIS NOTEBOOK COVER IS KNITTED IN COTTON IN A GARTER SLIP STITCH, WHICH GIVES A FAIR DEGREE OF CUSHIONING WITHOUT TOO MUCH STRETCH. IT MAKES GOOD USE OF SMALL AMOUNTS OF CONTRAST COLOR YARNS, WHICH IN THIS CASE WERE DYED AFTER SPINNING WITH FIBER-REACTIVE DYES. THE CASE COULD EQUALLY BE USED FOR A PORTABLE ELECTRONIC DEVICE SINCE THE COTTON YARNS USED AVOID POSSIBLE PROBLEMS WITH FLUFF GETTING INTO THE WORKS.

## Knitting pattern

First, knit a swatch using a needle size appropriate to your yarn, cast on 21 stitches, and work five repeats of the eight-row pattern (40 rows) as follows:

**Row 1:** (MC) Knit.
**Row 2:** (MC) Knit.
**Row 3:** (CC1) Sl1 pwise wyab, *k1, sl1 pwise wyab, repeat from * to end.
**Row 4:** (CC1) Sl1 pwise wyif, *k1 sl1 pwise wyif, repeat from * to end.
**Row 5:** (MC) Knit.
**Row 6:** (MC) Knit.
**Row 7:** (CC2) *K1, sl1 pwise wyab, repeat from * to last st, k1.
**Row 8:** (CC2) *K1 sl1 pwise wyif, repeat from * to last st, k1. Cont to work using MC on rows 1–2 and 5–6 but work rows 3–4 and 7–8 as folls.
**Second repeat:** Work rows 3–4 in CC3, rows 7–8 in CC4.
**Third repeat:** Work rows 3–4 in CC5, rows 7–8 in CC1.
**Fourth repeat:** Work rows 3–4 in CC2, rows 7–8 in CC3.
**Fifth repeat:** Work rows 3–4 in CC4, rows 7–8 in CC5.
**Note:** The color changes are not important for the sample and for planning the project quantities, but if used will help you decide if your proposed color combinations look pleasing.

Next, measure the swatch and make a note of the dimensions. Measure the item (notebook, iPad etc.) that the cover is to fit. Figure the number of stitches to cast on according to the length (longer dimension) of the item. Round up to an odd number of stitches. Figure the number of rows that equate to the circumference (around the shorter dimension) of the item.

Before going further, check that either you have enough yarn to complete the project or that you have access to more fiber if you may need to spin a little more (see page 132). MC accounts for approximately two-thirds of the total yarn required and CC yarn one-third. The project shown has five contrast colors.

Now, cast on an odd number of stitches for your project as previously figured and, following the stitch pattern and changing contrast colors each time, knit a piece long enough to fit the circumference of your item, finishing with two rows of MC, then bind off.

To make up, refer to the diagram, right. First sew together the cast-on and bound-off edges AB to CD, then sew up the right selvage E to BD to form a side seam (this is the side with the yarn tails from the color changeovers).

Finally, make a button loop of single crochet stitches or knit a loop by casting on and binding off the stitches on the next row. Secure the button to the center of the top edge.

## >> Equipment

- Knitting needles
- Tape measure
- Tapestry needle
- Crochet hook (optional)

## >> Yarns

These two-ply yarns are spun worsted-style directly from a natural cotton sliver. If you find it hard to spin cotton thickly enough, consider making a three-ply or cabled yarn instead. In addition to the yarn, you will also need a button to make a fastening.

## >> Project details

**Size:** 8 x 10½in (20 x 27cm)

**Yarn one (MC):** cream handspun
**Fiber:** natural cotton sliver
**Spun as:** worsted-style two-ply
**Wraps per inch:** 15 (6 wpc)
**Yards per pound:** 800yd/lb (1600m/kg)
**Quantity of MC yarn:** 80yd; 1½oz (70m; 45g)

**Yarn two (CC):** five shades: rose; pink; green; purple; yellow handspun. Yarns are as yarn one, dyed after spinning with fiber-reactive dyes.
**Fiber:** cotton sliver
**Spun as:** worsted-style two-ply
**Wraps per inch:** 15 (6 wpc)
**Yards per pound:** 800yd/lb (1600m/kg)
**Quantity of CC yarn:** 50yd, 1oz (45m, 30g)

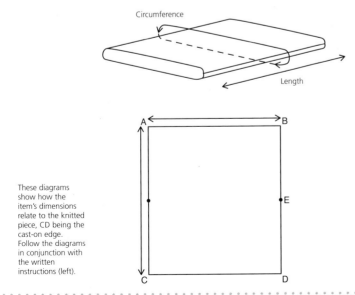

Circumference

Length

A ──────────────────► B

E

C ──────────────────── D

These diagrams
show how the
item's dimensions
relate to the knitted
piece, CD being the
cast-on edge.
Follow the diagrams
in conjunction with
the written
instructions (left).

**ABBREVIATIONS**

**k:** knit

**p:** purl

**sl1 pwise:** slip the stitch from the left to
the right needle, as if to purl it, but
without doing so

**wyab:** with the yarn at the back of the
needle (as when knitting)

**wyif:** with the yarn in front of the
needle (as when purling)

**MC:** main color

**CC:** contrast color

**CC1,2,3,4,5:** contrast color 1,2,3,4,5
respectively

**folls:** follows

**\*:** start of a repeat

# Chapter 5

# Professional approaches

This chapter takes you to the next level and aims to provide rational answers to the question "how can you justify acquiring yet more fiber?" It also covers essential planning and record-keeping and features an inspirational gallery of work by internationally renowned spinners.

# Going commercial

IT IS UNLIKELY THAT YOU WILL BE ABLE TO SUPPORT YOURSELF FINANCIALLY BY HAND SPINNING YARN ALONE, HOWEVER EXPERT AND PRODUCTIVE YOU BECOME. THERE ARE MANY MORE FACETS TO "GOING COMMERCIAL" THAN MAKING YOUR ENTIRE LIVING FROM YOUR SPINNING OUTPUT. HERE ARE SOME SUGGESTIONS TO START YOU OFF.

Hand spinning feels so good that it can become almost an addiction. You may be tempted to acquire more and more fiber, so it makes sense to think of ways to allow you to continue to spin more and more yarn with a clear conscience.

## Pricing

There are different approaches to pricing your work for sale. For example, you can start with the hourly amount of money you think you should earn. Factor in how long it takes you to prepare the fiber and spin a standard quantity of yarn, add on your raw materials cost and other relevant costs, and come up with the price you need to charge for your yarn. A totally different approach would be to look at the price per pound (or per kilo) of commercially-spun yarns and set a price in relation to that. In my view, neither of these is wholly realistic.

The first price, based on your desired hourly earnings, will mostly make your yarn sound so expensive that even the rich who can afford the price will be shocked. Prospective customers will be judging your product purely on the basis of what it seems like it should be worth, and if it took you too long to make it, they may think that's your problem rather than theirs. Your rate of production in ounces (or grams) per hour will vary more than yards (or meters) per hour between thick and thin yarns, so one thing to think about is to concentrate on thicker yarns and to start with clean, prepared fiber.

These colorful bobbins could make an eye-catching display, but realistically-priced fine plied yarns like these would be an expensive sales line.

*continued* ▶

| ESTIMATING TIME | Rate of work | Math | Time per 1oz |
|---|---|---|---|
| **Task: Dyeing** | | | |
| Dyeing 1lb of fiber | 80 minutes to dye the batch | 80 minutes ÷ 16 ounces | 5 minutes |
| **Task: Spinning[1]** | | | |
| Spinning first singles | 2yd per minute | 50yd ÷ 2yd per minute | 25 minutes |
| Spinning second singles | 2yd per minute | 50yd ÷ 2yd per minute | 25 minutes |
| Plying | 5yd per minute | 50yd ÷ 5yd per minute | 10 minutes |
| **Total time** | | | 65 minutes |

| DIRECT MATERIALS COSTS | Price paid | Math | $ per 1oz |
|---|---|---|---|
| Item: 1lb of prepared fiber | $32 | $32 ÷ 16 ounces | $2 |
| Item: dyestuffs to dye 10lb of prepared fiber | $40 | $40 ÷ 10lb ÷ 16 ounces | $0.25 |
| **Total materials costs** | | | $2.25 |

| FINAL COSTING CALCULATION | | Math | $ per 1oz |
|---|---|---|---|
| Direct materials costs | | See above | $2.25 |
| Time based costs[2] | | 65 ÷ 60 minutes = 1.083 hours @ $10 / hour | $10.83 |
| **Total cost** | | | $13.08 |

This sample calculation shows you, with some simple numbers and bold assumptions, how you could translate your direct costs and the time it takes you into a cost price per ounce, which you could then round up to the price to charge. It takes no account of other factors such as marketing overheads and retail margin.

**Assumptions**

[1] The yarn you are spinning yields 50yds/oz (800yds/lb)

[2] You wish to earn $10 per hour for your time

This website features a range of yarns and wearables based on a harmonious collection with a clear link to the inspiration. The puns in the tagline ("ply away home" and "for a luxuriously textured life") add personality to the craft on display.

## Writing a yarn description for your website

You have put a lot of care and effort into producing your yarn, so you owe it to yourself to mark its birth properly by giving it a name—and buyers love names. It also helps to clearly identify which yarn is which when speaking to a prospective customer, rather than "the one half way down on the left with a bit of blue in it." The name should hint at the inspiration for the yarn, and a few words about the particular inspiration for the yarn all help to build up the value image of the yarn and the thought you put into its creation.

You should always include specific data for the yarn, thinking about it from the perspective of a buyer who is probably not a spinner personally. Technicalities like twists per inch, Z- and S-twist direction, etc., are probably not for them; total weight and total length definitely are, translate this into yards per pound (or m/kg) as well as a general description of the relative yarn weight: lace-weight, sport-weight, bulky etc. If your yarn is likely to appeal to knitters, it's also a good idea to suggest a needle gauge for knitting, and to suggest an end use for the yarn.

And why not take a leaf out of the book of the internet giants who have made web selling an artform by including a note of "You might also like..." and a cross reference to another of your yarns, kits, products, or services.

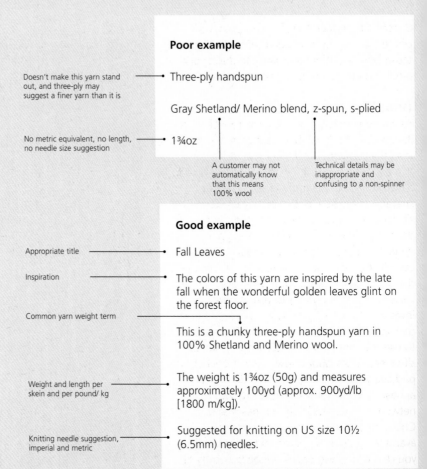

**Poor example**

Doesn't make this yarn stand out, and three-ply may suggest a finer yarn than it is → Three-ply handspun

Gray Shetland/ Merino blend, z-spun, s-plied

No metric equivalent, no length, no needle size suggestion → 1¾oz

A customer may not automatically know that this means 100% wool

Technical details may be inappropriate and confusing to a non-spinner

**Good example**

Appropriate title → Fall Leaves

Inspiration → The colors of this yarn are inspired by the late fall when the wonderful golden leaves glint on the forest floor.

Common yarn weight term → This is a chunky three-ply handspun yarn in 100% Shetland and Merino wool.

Weight and length per skein and per pound/ kg → The weight is 1¾oz (50g) and measures approximately 100yd (approx. 900yd/lb [1800 m/kg]).

Knitting needle suggestion, imperial and metric → Suggested for knitting on US size 10½ (6.5mm) needles.

Basing your price on a commercial equivalent is equally problematic. Whatever price you fix on, you should always do the math of the net amount, after expenses, you will earn per hour. You don't want to learn, down the line, that you have accidentally exploited yourself.

My strong recommendation for pricing your work is that you charge no less than the amount the market will stand, having done a little research. This can certainly take into account the fact that, as a beginner, your product quality may not yet be that great, but that is not to say that your yarn will be uninteresting to potential buyers as a result. Many craftspeople of all disciplines are very dependent on the money they can raise from their sales, and you owe it to them not to undercut their prices casually without thinking of the consequences. A significant price tag, to those who can afford it, is likely to make your product more, rather than less, desirable.

## Branding

As with selling any product, a smartly branded item is likely to do so much better in the market than the one with no planned brand identity. You are not going to be in the position of hiring a leading media agency to create your branding strategy and image, but it will pay dividends to sit down and give the matter a little quality thought. Think about a name, a design, or symbol that epitomizes your product range and can differentiate it from others. Bear in mind the brand qualities you want it to have, and the values that are important to you. Having invested your time in this way (precious time that you could have spent spinning), remember to use your brand identity consistently and in all situations. Think about how you will label and package your products, how the identity will appear on your website, your blog, social networking sites, and your business cards. Check out whether your brand name is available as a domain name and register it if you can, which also opens up the possibility of a personalized email address such as

▶

## Branding your work

Atmospheric photography symbolizes this brand image (above) yet the labels could be printed on your home equipment.

The typography on the business card (left) has evolved, but there is still a strong style linkage with the other materials.

yourname@yourbrand.com. All of this may seem a little too grandiose for modest ambitions of selling a little handspun yarn to feed your spinning habit, but it costs little to register a domain and even less to do a little thinking before taking action.

## Craft fairs

Selling at craft fairs is a great way to make contact with your clients on a face-to-face basis: they can touch your lovely yarns and express their undying admiration for your skill and patience. But before you can make this direct contact with prospective clients, they have to want to come to your table or into your booth. One surefire attraction is to sit demonstrating spinning. That will get you noticed and it's easy to smile and then strike up a conversation with passers-by. Ask them if they are familiar with hand-spinning; ask if they knit; ask if they can guess what fiber you are spinning. Above all, give them permission to touch!

Make your area look neat: a black cloth covering the table will make a great background for pale or colored yarns, and it should be long enough to reach down to the floor so that you can keep all your sundries out of sight and give a clean and tidy look to the booth. Have a visitors book and pen on view and ask anyone interested in your work to leave their contact details so you can drop them an email to let them know if you have produced a new line or if you have another craft fair coming up. When you make sales, record the buyer's contact information on the sales receipt.

## Labeling

Getting labels commercially printed is likely to be disproportionately expensive, so think about how you can use your home facilities to produce lovely keepsake-type labels. They can be totally handmade, with the details handwritten for a truly personal touch, or you can use your computer printer to produce adhesive labels for attachment to heavier weight card. I think skeins are lovely for display purposes, though as your customers might not have access to a swift and ball winder, you might offer a ball winding service for a small extra fee.

Include both the weight and approximate length of the yarn, a suggestion of suitable needle size if the yarn is for knitting, and washing instructions. And, of course, include your own brief contact details so that your customers can come back for more.

## Photographing your yarns for sales purposes

In any circumstances when you are selling (other than in a face-to-face situation with your customer), you are going to be reliant on an image and description of your yarn or completed article. Choose a good neutral background that contrasts well with your yarn.

Right: Subtle color interactions would make this chunky yarn an attractive selling line.

Left: A very neat craft show booth with all the clutter out of sight and the yarns arranged in a beautiful color spectrum.

Mid-gray is a safe choice, since it contrasts well with white or pale colors and gives a jewel-like contrast to strong colors. If none of your colors are dark, then black is a great choice for the background. If you are shooting a series of work, using the same photography style for everything gives a sense of cohesion and will make your work look more like a unified range.

Your photos probably don't need lots of megapixels, but they do need to be bright, in focus, and not blurred. Without access to professional photography lighting equipment, try shooting in good daylight—overcast rather than sunny, so as to avoid harsh shadows. Use a tripod if you have one and take the picture on the delay setting to avoid camera shake. If you are not using a delay setting, make sure you give the camera time to set its autofocus on the first half-press of the button—rushing can give a poor out-of-focus result. Finally, use your photo-editing software to crop or straighten the images, and you will have a great result that will do justice to your lovely yarns.

## Selling online

The advantage of selling online is that you can potentially reach a massive audience at very low cost. But note the word "potentially" and remember that the one thing people want to do when presented in the flesh with a skein of handspun yarn is to feel it—rather difficult to replicate online.

You may be put off thinking that you have to set up your own website and go into the finer points of e-commerce to make headway with selling online, but networks such as Etsy and  ▶

CONTENT:

AMOUNT:

PRICE:

SHEPHERD'S MOON    LLEGAD Y BUGAIL

**HANDSPUN BY ELLEN ROBERTS**

WWW.SHEPHERDSMOON.COM

**Girl with a Hook**

www.girlwithahook.com

Above: An elegantly simple yarn label capturing basic yarn data and the all-important web contact details. Left: An utterly simple but extremely strong brand image that speaks clearly to the intended audience.

Ravelry have come together to make it much less scary. Etsy describes itself as "more than a marketplace: we're a community of artists, creators, collectors, thinkers, and doers." As a marketplace, however, you are in the company of like-minded people who are much more likely to appreciate and value the handmade qualities of your product than the average buyer looking for a low-price bargain on a general auction site. Getting started is easy—just click on the "Sell" link to read all about the procedure and fees that apply. Don't forget to research the prices of other yarns and handspun projects before making your own listing. Ravelry is a very popular free site for knitters and crocheters where there are many networking opportunities for linking up with like-minded people and inserting paid advertisements.

## Accepting commissions

Another way of getting paid for your spinning time is to accept a commission to spin fiber for others. This can be a tricky area to navigate, but is worth considering. Make sure the time you will need to spend on the work is going to be genuinely pleasurable as well, and that the work will not go on so long and prove to be boring. One possibility is to make sure you can walk away from the commission if it ends up making you miserable.

Before you can price a commission, you will need to know exactly what's involved in terms of fiber preparation and the specification of the yarn required, such as how many plies and the thickness. Refer to the paragraphs on pricing your work for ideas on how to price spinning to commission. It could be easier for you to price by the yard (or meter) rather than by weight, but your client may find it easier to think in terms of weight. You can't give a realistic price by weight, however, until you have assessed (and preferably spun a small sample of) the fiber and agreed on the yarn type and grist.

You may find that requests find their way to you involving the spinning of pet hair. Taking a purely commercial view, it might be advisable to steer clear of such requests and try to let the

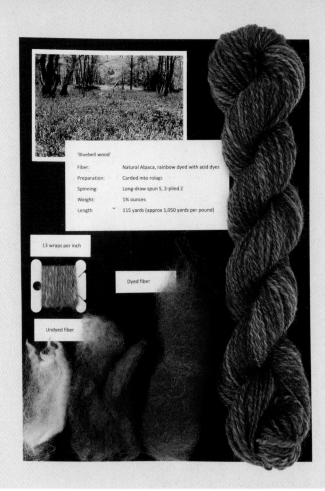

A competition entry showing the inspiration and transition from raw fiber to finished skein. The yarn data is clearly and succinctly stated.

inquirer down as gently as possible. I strongly suggest you don't take on a commission to spin pet hair at all until you have had the opportunity to spin a sample. If you do want to spin someone's pet hair, a blend with another fiber such as wool is often much more successful than the hair on its own, so consider suggesting that to the client.

Another commission to be wary of is a request to spin a large quantity of fleece in return for being able to keep just a proportion of it. As this request rarely seems to be related to the finest de-haired cashmere, it is normally severely out of balance in value terms—politely turn it down unless a manageable quantity is involved.

## Collaborating

Your beautiful handspun yarns will be very precious to you, and they will also be precious to other craftspeople. If you are a maker at heart, and you will probably not be reading this book unless you have a fundamental desire to make things, you will probably have a number of other makers in your social circle, many of them involving textile crafts. Collaborating on joint projects could be a great way forward.

Your knitting and crochet friends who don't spin will be over the moon to be offered some beautiful handspun yarns to incorporate into a project, doubly so if you plan the collaboration in advance of the spinning and of specifying the project. This will be a stimulating two-way dialogue about what the yarn possibilities are, what the project possibilities are, and how both can be shaped through discussion and sampling—the whole will undoubtedly be greater than the sum of the parts.

Weaving tends to be yarn-hungry. Going back in time to when all yarn had to be handspun and hand-woven for ordinary domestic consumption, it took several spinners to keep up with the needs of one weaver. But the inclusion of some handspun yarn as an accent is a different matter altogether. A hand-weaver would normally be delighted to have access to some custom-spun yarn; this greatly expands the possibilities and gives a further dimension to the hand-woven fabric that the two of you have jointly created.

## Competitions

Although some competitions carry a monetary prize, the real plus of winning a spinning competition is the boost it will give to your reputation—something you will, of course, mention in your blog and on your website. Competitions are great fun and enable you to concentrate on spinning to a brief. Read the rules well and, a bit like exams in school and college, make sure you answer the precise question. For example, if the rules say that a skein must be within a particular weight range, your beautiful spinning will be disqualified if the skein is too heavy or too light. Present your spinning as beautifully as possible, accompanied by a smart data sheet, a fiber sample, and the inspiration as applicable.

Look for details in the classified listings in spinning magazines and get organized well ahead of time so that it is not a last minute scramble to meet the submission deadline.

## Teaching

When you have acquired a fine skill such as the art of spinning, it is hugely rewarding to pass it on to others as well as potentially earning a monetary reward for your time. New spinners benefit greatly from one-to-one help, and with the upsurge in knitting there is quite a demand for spinning tutors. Inquiries often come simply by word of mouth through a group such as a spinning guild, so make it known to your guild friends that you would be happy to provide instruction. Fiber and yarn stores sometimes offer classes, so let your local stores know that you are available to teach, either in their own classes or you could offer individual follow-up instruction to students who have taken an introductory class.

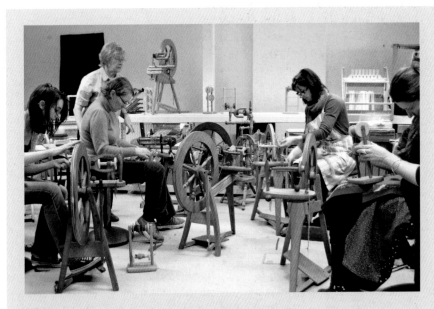

Above: Teaching at a yarn or fiber store normally means that a number of wheels are available. This group for beginners is deep in concentration. Image courtesy of The Handweavers Studio & Gallery, London.

# Planning and record-keeping

IF YOU ARE SPINNING FOR A SPECIFIC PROJECT, PARTICULARLY A LARGE PROJECT SUCH AS A KNITTED SWEATER, YOU DON'T WANT TO GET A LONG WAY INTO KNITTING ONLY TO FIND YOU HAVE RUN OUT OF YARN AND CANNOT REPEAT THE SAME BATCH OF FIBER. SO, JUST AS IF YOU WERE FOLLOWING A COMMERCIAL KNITTING PATTERN, YOU NEED AN IDEA OF HOW MUCH YARN YOU ARE GOING TO NEED.

## Expert advice

**Accurate weighing method**
Measure and record the exact length and width of the swatch and make a note of how many rows and stitches it contains. Next, work out its area (simply multiply the length and width together). If you have very accurate scales that can weigh very small amounts, weigh the swatch and make a note of the precise weight reading. Next, work out the weight of the swatch per unit area—do this by dividing the weight of the swatch by its area.

Finally, estimate the area of your knitted project by measuring the existing item. Then the weight of yarn you need equals the area of the project multiplied by the weight per unit area of the swatch.

You can work this out as the total length or the total weight, but when you are buying fiber, it's the weight that you need to know. If you have a very similar item that is the right dimensions and knitted with a similar stitch in the same thickness and type of yarn, a good starting point is simply to weigh the existing item. You can make a pretty good estimate even when not all of these things hold true. Always add a good margin for error—especially when you are a beginner—as your spinning thickness may vary. Start by spinning a sample skein and knitting a sample swatch measuring about 4in (10cm) in each direction in your chosen stitch pattern, trying different needle sizes to get the right feel.

## Measured skein method
This method can be used when you don't have such accurate scales. When you make a skein on a niddy noddy, simply count the number of turns you make, measure the length of one turn, multiply by the number of turns, and record the total length of the finished skein. If you have a number of skeins to be used together, record the sum of their lengths. Weigh the skein or skeins as accurately as you can and record the total weight. Finally, work out the average number of yards per ounce or meters per gram (total length divided by total weight). Commercial yarn sizes are usually given as yards per pound or meters per kilogram, and if you wish to convert between the two, the conversion factor is almost precisely 2, that is, the number of yards per pound is approximately half the meters per kilogram.

When making your swatch, measure and mark a point on the yarn exactly 1yd (or 1m) from the knitting needles, and carry on knitting while counting how many stitches you get per yard or per meter. The total number of stitches in the sample is the number of stitches per row, multiplied by the number of rows.

Next, work out the total length of yarn in the sample (total number of stitches in the swatch divided by number of stitches per yard or per meter).

Earlier you recorded the number of yards per ounce or meters per gram, and now you also know total length in the sample, so your next step is to work out the accurate weight of the sample as a fraction of an ounce or gram (divide the length of the sample by the yards per ounce or by the meters per gram). As before, work out the weight per unit area of the swatch. Finally, the total weight of yarn you need for your project equals the area of the project multiplied by the weight per unit area of the swatch.

## Final check
As you spin each skein, record its length and add up the total length of yarn spun for the project for comparison with the total length you should need, worked out as follows. You know how many stitches per yard or meter, and also how many stitches in the sample, so you can work out the total length used in the sample. You also know its area. So the total length you should need is (total area of project) divided by (area of sample) multiplied by (length in the sample). This should be a closer estimate than your earlier calculations of weight of fiber needed, but still allow something extra as a margin for error.

If you don't have quite enough, and you can't spin more of the same, make an adjustment now rather than meet with disappointment later. For instance, plan for shorter sleeves, or incorporate some contrast yarn as an accent.

## McMorran balance

A McMorran balance is a device for measuring the count of a yarn (yards per pound or meters per kilo) directly. It is calibrated to balance when a precise weight of yarn is on the balance arm; the length of yarn which balances then relates directly to its count.

**1** Place the balance near the edge of the table and put a sample of yarn in the arm of the balance that will weigh it down. Make sure it hangs free of the table edge.

**2** With sharp scissors, repeatedly trim the ends of the yarn sample until the arm just balances.

**3** Measure the length of yarn you are left with and consult the information provided with the balance for how to read off the yarn count from the length. Separate devices are sold with either imperial or metric calibrations. With my imperial version, 100 times the number of inches in the sample length equals the number of yards per pound.

## Spinning for a project—record sheet

This format aims to capture all the key numbers you need to plan a project with confidence. Take photocopies of this page for your own use.

| | |
|---|---|
| **Sample swatch:** no. of stitches ...... x no. of rows ...... = .......... total stitches | |
| width ..... x length ..... = ........... area of swatch | |
| Needles used ............  Stitch pattern ..... | |
| Stitches per yard/meter ..... | |
| Length used in swatch ..... | |
| Accurate weight of swatch .....  (measured or calculated) | |
| Area of project .....  square inches/square centimeters | |
| Calculated weight of yarn needed ..... | |
| Calculated length of yarn needed ..... | |

| One turn around the niddy noddy measures | | ..... yd/m | |
|---|---|---|---|
| | | Optional, but useful if you want to check your consistency | |
| Skein | Total length | Total weight | Yd/lb (m/kg) |
| 1. | | | |
| 2. | | | |
| 3. | | | |
| 4. | | | |
| 5. | | | |
| 6. | | | |
| 7. | | | |
| 8. | | | |
| 9. | | | |
| 10. | | | |
| 11. | | | |
| 12. | | | |
| 13. | | | |
| 14. | | | |
| Total | | | |

◀ Ode to Itten
**Brenda Gibson**
(www.brendagibson.com)
This yarn collection was inspired by
the color theory books of Johannes
Itten. Here, Brenda took the
complementary colors of yellow and
violet and blended proportions of
those two colors using mini combs to
produce intermediate neutral tones.
They are worsted-spun from the wool
of Masham sheep, and dyed in the
fleece using acid dyes.

# Gallery

THIS SECTION SHOWCASES WORK BY A RANGE OF
ACCOMPLISHED SPINNERS AND, IN SOME CASES, THE
WORK IS THE RESULT OF EFFECTIVE COLLABORATIONS.
THE STYLES FEATURED DIFFER WIDELY AND ARE SURE TO
INSPIRE YOU.

## Skeins

Although a skein may be said to be an intermediate phase in the
transition from fiber to finished article, there are few things as
lovely as a beautifully presented skein. Just think of the ways
these wonderful yarns could be applied to projects of your own.

◀ Faerie tale
**Naomi Ryono**
(www.knottynaomi.etsy.com)
The skein was a collaboration between Naom
Ryono and Lynn Wigell (*The Yarn Wench*). It
contains Coopworth, Cotswold, Romney, mok
locks, and Falkland. After spinning the single
thick thin, Naomi plied it with two strands: si
flowers on thread and weaving yarn. To add
more texture, she picked a complementary ba
fabric and novelty yarns and cut them into str
to spin with the batt before plying.

### ◀Raspberry truffle
**Riin Gill**
(www.happyfuzzyyarn.com)
Riin dyed a Blue-faced Leicester combed top in shades of brown, coral, and magenta, then split the top lengthwise into four strips before spinning with a modified long-draw technique. The two plies are the same. The skein is a typical worsted weight.

### ▶Harvest season
**Naomi Ryono**
(www.knottynaomi.estsy.com)
The fiber here is Blue-faced Leicester. Naomi spun the yarn as a two-ply with both plies of equal weight.

### Pocket full of poppies
hley Martineau
w.neauveau.com; www.shopneauveau.com)
s is a handspun thick and thin single ply yarn
h poppy flowers added in. Ashley spun this yarn
m an art batt she carded with kettle-dyed and
ural-colored fibers. Art batts are freeform
ded blends of fibers including hand-painted
ol, silk, mohair, alpaca, and sparkle. She carded
fibers once to leave plenty of texture from the
ural wool crimp and curl. She also used luxury
ers (cashmere, camel) that she recycled from
aveled wool sweaters. She attached the flowers
threading 3in (7.5cm) wool tufts through the
derside of each flower. As she spun the yarn
m the art batt, she took one flowered wool tuft,
n the wool tuft into the yarn, and secured the
ds of the wool tuft with fiber.

### ◀Persimmon embers
**Teresa Clayton**
(www.thetreadler.etsy.com)
A medium-grade wool with a staple length of approx. 3in (7.6cm). The fiber was acid dyed a bright orange and handspun thick and thin. The resulting yarn was then unevenly plied around a commercial cotton yarn. This technique has been called coils, beehives, midlife crisis twist (as spinning in this way purposefully breaks all the rules of well-tempered, evenly-tensioned plying to create an interesting bobbled texture in the finished yarn). A metallic blue thread was twisted into the yarn as it was plied and wound onto the bobbin for an added flash of sparkle.

### ▶Pirate's plunder
**Teresa Clayton**
(www.thetreadler.etsy.com)
Avast Ye! A wide sampling of the spinster's stash was plundered here to make this treasure trove of a knittin' yarrrrnnnn. Shades of copper, bronze, silver, and gold were flung together and given the heave-ho through ye old drum carder with no concern fer life ner limb resulting in a smooth yet motley batt for spinning. A fine, pewter wool yarn was then forced to "walk the plank" alongside the frey ensnarling itself into the booty. Shiver me timbers!

### ▼Winter frost
**Sue Macniven**
(www.handspunexotics.co.uk)
This yarn was spun as a competition piece for The Royal Highland Show where it won first prize in the fancy yarn section and the Mabel Ross memorial prize. Sue used a single of *Bombyx mori* silk and a carded blend of kid mohair and Angelina sparkle. The silk was over-twisted and then threaded with glass beads. The beads were moved along the yarn as it was plied and the silk twisted back on itself to make a "tail" with the bead in the end. The result is a cold and icy look, and the beads give the impression of little icicles.

### ▲Silent movie matinee
**Teresa Clayton**
(www.thetreadler.etsy.com)
An experiment in black and white wool, these fibers were lightly hand carded then drafted together to incorporate shades of gray during the spinning of a thick and thin yarn. Here, the same plying process utilized to make "Persimmon embers" on page 135 resulted in an interestingly spotted, "Op Art" effect in the finished yarn. Plied with a commercially spun manmade fiber.

### ▲Marmalade
**Rachel Jones**
(www.ontheround.etsy.com;
ontheround.blogspot.com)
This is a handspun two-ply thick and thin skein of yarn. The wool from this skein was hand blended on a drum carder only once to show off the chunks of luxury fibers. Fibers used in this skein include: Merino wool, Cormo fleece, banana fiber, Rambouillet fleece, tussah silk noil, soy silk, Firestar, Angelina fiber, and mohair locks. To spin this batt, Rachel ripped off chunks of the fiber and spun it without drafting to preserve the texture. The single was then plied making this a bulky yarn filled with textural surprises.

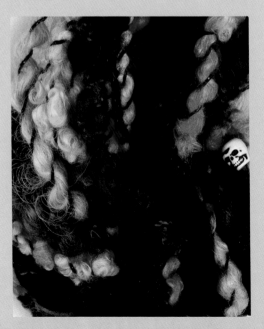

### ◄Punky
**Naomi Ryono**
(www.knottynaomi.etsy.com)
This handspun art yarn was spun from uncarded Blue-faced Leicester (BFL) locks that were plied with metallic yarn and skull beads.

## ◄Darkwing
**Eling Chang**
**(www.rhinofluff.com)**
This is a hand-dyed Merino wool top.
The combed wool top is split into lots of
strips and selected at random to form
lots of candy-cane striping and color
blends. The yarn is spun thick and thin
for texture. The bulkiness of the yarn
helps in highlighting the softness of the
Merino fibers, and the simple spinning
emphasizes the effect of the colors.

### ►Taste the rainbow
**Amanda Huntington**
**(www.mandalinn.etsy.com)**
This handspun plied yarn was spun
from "Rainbow Connection" batts
containing Blue-faced Leicester,
superwash Merino, Targhee wool,
and Angelina.

## ►Corkscrews and curlicues
**Teresa Clayton**
**(www.thetreadler.etsy.com)**
The same fibers that were used in "Silent
Movie Matinee," opposite, were blended
more thoroughly here during the carding
and drafting process for a less dramatic
effect. The fibers were then spun in much
the same way, only with a good deal of
excess twist purposefully incorporated
during the plying phase. This excess twist
was used to cable the yarn by plying it back
onto itself. The finished skein is a balanced
yarn with double the curlicues throughout,
creating a fun seashell effect.

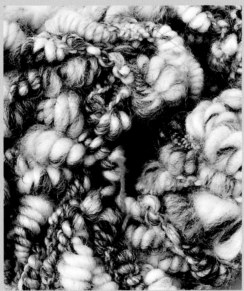

### ▼Kristina
**Riin Gill**
**(www.happyfuzzyyarn.com)**
In this skein, Riin dyed a Blue-faced
Leicester combed top in two different
colorways; one for each ply. As you
can see, one ply is blues and greens;
the other is pinks, oranges, and a light
aqua, which unifies the two plies. She
split the top into four strips before
spinning using a short-draw. The skein
is a bulky weight.

### ◄Ocean surf
**Eling Chang**
**(www.rhinofluff.com)**
This example is a mix of hand-dyed
and hand-carded wools, plus soy silk
and mohair. The fiber was carded to
blend colors for a heathered effect,
and the yarn was spun as a slightly
thick and thin single to show off the
texture of the different fibers. Colors
were chosen to reflect the colors of
ocean surf and sand.

# Wearables

The wonderful articles featured here encapsulate everything discussed in this book: the spinning, dyeing, planning, and beautiful execution. Now that you can create exactly the yarn of your choice, and know how to plan and figure out the quantities of fiber and yarn you need, all you need is inspiration. Look no further...

## ▼Pin-striped peplum
**Sarah C. Swett**
(www.sarah-swett.com)
This Cormo fleece from Montana, USA, was prepared on Russian paddle combs. The singles were spun semi-worsted in the Z direction and four-ply in the S direction on a Lendrum Saxony wheel. The finished yarn is about 16 wraps per inch (6 wpc). Several different colors were dyed in the skein using indigo, weld, madder, and cochineal. The black color is a combination of natural brown and indigo. The sweater was knitted in the round with a steek above the peplum.

## ▼Peruvian blue
**Sue Macniven**
(www.handspunexotics.co.uk)
This Peruvian-inspired hat was made to fit a child's head. The primary yarn is angora (dyed in different shades of green), with a blend of wool and silk. The earflaps are finished with Peruvian ceramic beads and the hat crowned with tassels.

**◄Purple haze**
**Sue Macniven**
**(www.handspunexotics.co.uk)**
Sue spun this hat for winter fishing in
Scotland, so it had to be warm and cozy
but not too garish. She used angora
rabbit, a carded blend of purple silk and
wool, and some highlights of kid mohair
and silk. The tassels were finished with
Peruvian ceramic beads.

## Rose and cream shawl
en Roberts
www.shepherdsmoon.co.uk)
s shawl is made up of 50–50 Merino/tussah
k. Ellen tie-dyed the Merino in black cherry-
vor Kool-Aid and handspun it as a singles. She
un a separate singles bobbin of tussah silk and
ed the two together on a Majacraft Rose
nning wheel. The pattern used in this garment
Marianne Kinzel's Azaela pattern (from her *Book*
*Modern Lace Knitting*). Ellen took out one of
e repeats and knitted it back and forth to make
nto an open pentagon.

## ►Seafoam wrap
**Ellen Roberts**
**(www.shepherdsmoon.co.uk)**
This was Ellen's first time at hand
blending the fiber prior to spinning. The
75 percent Merino/25 percent bamboo
blend was handspun on a Majacraft
Rose spinning wheel. The pattern is
"seafoam," found in Barbara Walker's
book, *Treasury of Knitting Patterns*.

# Health and safety

BEFORE YOU BEGIN SPINNING, THERE ARE VARIOUS HEALTH AND SAFETY PRECAUTIONS YOU MUST FAMILIARIZE YOURSELF WITH AND ADHERE TO.

Protective goggles and dust masks can be bought at DIY or builders supply stores.

Always use a dust mask when working with dye powders.

Keep a separate pair of rubber gloves for dyeing to avoid possible contamination with foodstuffs in your kitchen.

## Unwashed fiber

You may be dealing with animal fiber as it is directly clipped from the back of the animal and, as I have heard it politely stated, it will have evidence of its outdoor lifestyle. This covers a multitude of possibilities: mud from a field, sweat (suint), natural grease (lanolin for sheep), traces of urine and feces as well as the larvae of ticks, fleas, etc., and deposits of chemicals that may have been used against infestation before clipping. Many spinners love to spin their fleece "in the grease" to take advantage of the natural lanolin as a spinning lubricant, though I think it's always a good idea to give the fleece a light wash to remove dirt whilst leaving some natural lanolin behind. In any event, make sure your inoculations against tetanus are up to date and be meticulous about washing your hands, especially before eating or touching food.

When demonstrating in public, it's a real no-no to have totally unwashed fleece that visitors can touch. If you want to show the remarkable color change before and after washing, make sure the unwashed fiber is not for touching. It's also good practice to have hand sanitizer on hand for use after touching greasy fleece.

## Allergies

Even something as innocuous as wool can cause reactions of varying degrees. Always be clear about the fiber content you are spinning so that those who need to do so can avoid contact.

Some fine fibers are difficult to lock securely into a yarn and may shed. Angora and mohair are examples that come to mind. Beware of the possibility of triggering an asthma attack in asthma sufferers with fly-away fibers.

## Dyeing

Dyestuffs are frequently supplied in powder form, and there are serious health dangers if they are inhaled. When working with dye powders, wear a dust mask and reseal powder containers when they have been used. One of the advantages of working with dyestuffs in solution is that it addresses the inhalation risk as well as being a convenience. Work in a well-ventilated area to avoid inhaling fumes from chemical reactions or simmering dyes.

Dyestuffs, mordants, and modifiers may be seriously toxic, so you should avoid contact with the skin and splashing into the eyes. Wear rubber gloves and protective goggles as applicable, and clean up any spillages. Never use the same vessels for dyeing as for food.

Many dye processes involve bringing the dye bath up to a simmer or boil or fixing the dye using steam. Make sure that a large dye vat is stable when hot to avoid scalding, and be especially careful when working with steam; a steam burn is much more serious than one from boiling water.

## Equipment

You will be well aware of the need to keep your own fingers clear of the rotating wheel (with its spokes) or flyer (with its hooks) of your spinning wheel, but small children are unaware of the dangers. Make sure children are supervised when you demonstrate in public and that those too small to understand cannot get close enough to lunge.

Carders and combs can puncture the skin and wool combs in particular could cause a nasty injury if dropped or trodden on. Keep all your equipment safely stowed out of harm's way and the tines of combs appropriately protected.

# Glossary

HERE IS YOUR GUIDE TO ALL THE USEFUL TERMINOLOGY USED
IN THIS BOOK.

**BALANCE**
When a plied yarn has no residual
tendency to twist in either direction.

**BATT**
Carded preparation of fiber as
removed from hand carders or a
drum carder.

**BLOCKING**
Setting the twist of yarn or setting
the stitches of knitting.

**BOBBIN**
Spool, as mounted on a spinning
wheel.

**BRADFORD COUNT**
System of grading the fineness of
wool—the higher the number, the
finer the wool.

**CABLE**
Compound plied yarn (normally
four-ply) in which plied yarns are
further plied with each other in the
reverse direction.

**CARDING**
Spinning preparation process for
woolen spinning using either hand
carders or a drum carder in which
different length fibers are retained.

**CLOVE KNOT**
Common type of knot formed of
two half-hitches round an object.

**COMBING**
Spinning preparation process for
worsted spinning using wool combs
in which shorter fibers are removed
leaving only longer fibers of a similar
length.

**COP**
Package of yarn as it is built up on a
hand spindle, normally conical in
shape.

**CRIMP**
Natural wave of many animal fibers.

**DOUBLE CUT/SECOND CUT**
Fleece fault comprising very short
noils of fiber resulting from a double
pass of the shears during the
shearing process.

**DRAFT**
Thinning out fibers to a desired
thickness either prior to or as part of
the spinning process.

**FELTING**
Process by which the scales on fibers
lock together and form a solid sheet
or mass.

**FLYER**
U-shaped device on a spinning
wheel that rotates to impart
spinning twist and winds the spun
yarn onto the bobbin.

**GREASE (IN THE GREASE)**
Natural lanolin present in wool-
bearing animals. Spinning with fiber
where the lanolin has not been
removed by scouring is known as
"spinning in the grease."

**GRIST**
Thickness of a yarn, typically
measured as wraps per inch.

**HALF-HITCH**
Simple and quick releasing knot
typically used in spinning to secure a
yarn to a spindle without a hook. It
can be formed by a single twist in a
loop of yarn.

**LAZY KATE**
Device used in plying to support
bobbins.

**LEADER**
Length of yarn attached to a bobbin
or spindle onto which the yarn is
joined.

**LOCK**
Small quantity of fibers in a fleece
that naturally cling lightly together.

**LONG-DRAW**
Technique for woolen-spun yarns by
which yarn is drafted and spun from
rolags an arm's length at a time.

**NAVAJO PLYING (CHAIN PLYING)**
Where a three-ply yarn is made
from one supply of singles by
making a large-scale crochet chain
with the fingers while adding plying
twist.

**NIDDY NODDY**
Device used for hand-winding skeins
of a constant length, consisting of a
central shaft and two shorter
crossbars at each end at right angles
to each other.

**NOILS**
Short tangles of fiber that, if left in
the fiber at the spinning stage, will
prevent a smooth yarn being spun.

**ORIFICE**
Hole through which the yarn
emerges from the flyer assembly
toward the hands of the spinner.

**ROLAG**
Rolled preparation of fiber for
woolen spinning made from a
carded batt.

**ROVING**
Parallel arrangement of combed
fibers for worsted spinning.

**SCOTCH TENSION**
System whereby the flyer is driven
by the wheel and the bobbin has its
own brake band.

**SHORT-DRAW**
Technique for worsted-spun yarns
by which yarn is drafted and spun a
few inches at a time, keeping the
hands close together and preventing
twist from entering the drafting
zone of unspun fibers.

**SKEIN**
Hank of yarn prior to being wound
into balls etc. Enables spun yarn to
be washed, dyed, and blocked.

**SLIVER**
Long bundle of untwisted fibers
prepared for spinning; when slightly
twisted it becomes a roving.

**SLUBS**
Unspun thick fibers in a spun yarn.

**SQUARE KNOT**
Simple and common double knot—
left over right, right over left. One
of its useful properties is that it can
be "collapsed" rather than untied.

**STAPLE**
Staple length is the fully extended
length of individual fibers before
spinning). A staple is an alternative
term for a lock.

**TIP**
Opposite end of the fiber from the
shorn cut end.

**TOP**
Commercial parallel combed fiber
preparation, available to hand-
spinners.

**WARP**
Thread, parallel to the selvage of the
cloth, that is mounted under tension
on a loom for weaving.

**WEFT**
Thread, at right angles to the
selvage of the cloth, that is carried
by a shuttle during weaving.

**WHORL**
Weighted disk on a hand spindle or
a pulley wheel on a spinning wheel.

**WOOLEN**
Spinning method, not necessarily
containing wool fiber, for a light
and airy yarn, potentially including
both shorter and longer fibers.

**WORSTED**
Spinning method, not necessarily
containing wool fiber, for a
compact, sleek yarn, containing
fibers of a uniform length.

**WRAPS**
Number of times a yarn can be
wound around something such as a
card or a ruler in a given length to
establish the grist of the yarn.

# Resources

THIS LIST IS ORGANIZED GEOGRAPHICALLY, BUT MANUFACTURERS
WILL NORMALLY HAVE LOCAL AGENTS, AND SUPPLIERS WILL GENERALLY
SHIP WORLDWIDE.

## AMERICAS

**Schacht Spindle Company, Inc.**
www.schachtspindle.com
Manufacturers of spinning and weaving
equipment.

**Webs (Valley Fibers Corporation)**
www.yarn.com
Fiber and equipment suppliers; classes
available.

**Abstract Fiber**
www.abstractfiber.com
Hand-painted fiber and yarn.

**The Fold**
www.thefoldatmc.net
Fiber and equipment suppliers; classes
available.

**K C L Woods**
www.kclwoods.com
Fine hand spindles and shuttles.

**Handweavers Guild of America**
www.weavespindye.org
For individual membership or Guild
affiliation.
Publishers of *Shuttle Spindle & Dyepot.*

**American Sheep Industry Association**
www.sheepusa.org

## EUROPE

**Louët BV**
www.louet.nl/en
Manufacturers of spinning and weaving
equipment.

**The Handweavers Studio & Gallery**
www.handweavers.co.uk
Fiber and equipment suppliers; classes
available.

**Wingham Wool Work**
www.winghamwoolwork.co.uk
Fiber and equipment suppliers; tuition and
fiber sampling available.

**Michael Williams Woodturner, Fine
Woodworker**
www.michael-williams-wood.co.uk
Fine hand spindles, spinning and weaving
accessories.

**Association of Guilds of Weavers,
Spinners & Dyers**
www.wsd.org.uk
Coordinating body of UK Guilds of
Weavers, Spinners & Dyers.
Publishers of *The Journal for Weavers,
Spinners & Dyers.*

**Kemtex Educational Supplies**
www.kemtex.co.uk
Suppliers of dyestuffs, auxiliary chemicals,
and kits.

**The Rare Breeds Survival Trust**
www.rbst.org.uk

**Brtish Wool Marketing Board**
www.britishwool.org.uk

## AUSTRALASIA

**Ashford Handicrafts**
www.ashford.co.nz
Manufacturers of spinning and weaving
equipment.

**Majacraft Ltd**
www.majacraft.co.nz
Manufacturers of spinning equipment.

**The Australian Forum for Textile Arts**
www.tafta.org.au
Publishers of *Textile Fibre Forum.*

# Index

Figures in *italics* indicate captions.

**A**
abaca 27
air-jet systems 12
allergies 140
alpaca 24, 44
angora 25, 140
Arkwright, Richard 12

**B**
balance 59, 64–65, 77
ball winding service 128
ball-winder 22, 23, 79, 128
balls
  center-pull balls 79
  creating solid balls 78
  nostepinne method 79
  plying from a center-pull ball 66
  twist influence 79
bamboo 26, 26, 44
bast fibers 26
batts
  carded 15, 35, 37, 56
  doffing 33
  drum-carded 37
  hand-carded 36
  removing 33
  shaded 34
  woolen-style 14
binder 71, 73
blending
  color 14, 34
  fibers 14, 35
blocking
  blocking balanced or almost balanced
    yarns 76
  blocking singles or over-twist yarns
    76
"bloom" 56, 77
blue-faced Leicester (BFL) wool 25
bobbin whorl 20
bobbins 20, 52
  plying from two bobbins 64–65
  storage 18
  thick core 60, 61
bouclé yarn 68, 71, 102–103
"bracelet" yarn 68–69
Bradford count 24
brake tension adjuster 20
branding 127–128, 127
break, dealing with a 66
Brown, Moses 12
bullion yarn 73
business cards 127

**C**
cable-plied yarn 70–71
camel 25
carding 14, 32–33
  drum 33
  hand 32
  health and safety 140
cashmere 25, 44
Cave of the Chimneys, San Miguel
  Island, USA 10
Chang, Eling 137
Clayton, Teresa 135, 136, 137
collaborating 130–131

combing 14, 34, 40–41, 54
  English wool combs 41
  health and safety 140
  using a dog comb 40
  using mini hand-combs 41
competitions 130, 131
cop 47
core yarn 71, 72, 73
corkscrew yarn 70
cotton 10, 26, 26, 42, 44
craft fairs 128, 128
Crompton, Samuel 13

**D**
direction 59
distaff 11
doffer 15
doffing the batt 33
dog comb 14, 15, 40
double drive band 18, 20, 53
doubled leader 46, 51
drafting rate 63
draining yarn 77
drive band 20, 53
  tension adjuster 20
drive wheel 20
drum carder 14, 15, 33, 56
drying yarn 77
dust mask 140, 140
dyeing 42–45
  fiber reactive dye: ingredients based
    on depth of shade 42
  fibre reactive dyes vs. acid dyes 42
  health and safety 140
  level dyeing with acid dyes 42–43
  level dyeing with fiber reactives dyes
    42–43
  rainbow dyeing 42, 44
  rainbow dyeing with acid dyes 44–45
  rainbow dyeing with fiber reactive
    dyes 44–45

**E**
electric spinners 12
Elizabeth, St, of Hungary 11
English wool combs 40, 41
equipment: health and safety 140
Etsy 130
evenness 62, 63

**F**
fairy tales 12, 13
fiber preparation tools 14, 14, 15
fibers 24–27
  animal 24, 24–25, 140
  cellulose 26, 42, 44
  plant 26, 26–27
  protein 26, 42, 44
  synthetic 26, 26–27
  unwashed 140
figure-eight ties 75
flax (linen) 12, 13, 14, 26, 44
flick carder 15
flyer 10, 11, 12, 13, 18, 20, 53
  jumbo 18, 18
  lace 18, 18, 60
flyer whorl 20
footman 20
"fulled" woven items 56

**G**
Gallery 134–139
  skeins 134–137
    *Corkscrews and curlicues* 137
    *Darkwing* 137
    *Faerie tale* 134
    *Harvest season* 135
    *Kristina* 137
    *Marmalade* 136
    *Ocean surf* 137
    *Ode to Itten* 134
    *Persimmon embers* 135
    *Pirate's plunder* 135
    *Pocket full of poppies* 135
    *Punky* 136
    *Raspberry truffle* 135
    *Silent movie matinee* 136
    *Taste the rainbow* 137
    *Winter frost* 136
  wearables 138–39
    *Peruvian blue* 138
    *Pin-striped peplum* 138
    *Purple haze* 139
    *Rose and cream shawl* 139
    *Seafoam wrap* 139
Gandhi, Mahatma 10, 11, 19
Gibson, Brenda 134
Gill, Riin 135, 137
ginning 26
glossary 141
goggles 14 0, 140
grease, spinning in the 30, 77, 140

**H**
hand carders 14, 14, 15, 32, 36
Happy Fuzzy Yarn 137
hat and mittens, knitted 112–116
health and safety 140
hemp 26
history of spinning 10–13
horsehair 25
Huntingdon, Amanda 137

**I**
ingeo 27
Irish tension 52, 53
Isle of Wight 10

**J**
Jacob sheep 24
Jones, Rachel 136
jute 27

**K**
kemp 24

**L**
labeling 128–129, 129
lazy kate 18, 22, 22, 64
leader yarn 46, 64
left-/right-handed 6
linen 27
long-bast fibers 14
long-draw technique 10, 12, 13, 19
  American long-draw spinning 56
  English long-draw spinning 57
loom weights 10
lyocell 26

**M**
McMorran balance 22, 23, 133
Macniven, Sue 136, 138, 139
Martineau, Ashley 135
mawata 24, 54
measured skein method 132
mechanization 12, 12, 13
microns 24
milk protein 27
mini combs 14, 15, 40, 41
mittens, knitted hat and 112–116
mohair 25, 44, 140
mule spinning machine 13

**N**
neps 62
nettle 26, 27
niddy-noddy 22, 22, 74, 76, 132
nostepinne 22, 22, 78, 79

**O**
orifice 20, 50, 51, 64

**P**
pet hair 130
petite niddy noddy 22
photography 127, 129
pillow cover, woven 110–111
planning and record-keeping 132–133
plying
  Andean 68–69
  conventional 64–66
  direction 59
  fancy yarn 70–73
  from a center-pull ball 66
  from spindles 49
  from two bobbins 64–65
  Navajo (chain) 67
plying and yarn handling tools 22–23
pom pom maker 116
pre-drafting 38–39
  pre-drafting a commercial top 38
  splitting a top into "fingers" 39
pricing your work for sale 124–125,
  127, 128
projects
  knitted hat and mittens 112–116
  knitted slipcase 120–121
  tassels 117–119
  Woven pillow cover 110–111
public liability insurance cover 128
punis 14, 36
  making 37

**R**
ramie 27, 44
Ravelry 130
record sheet 133
resources 142
retting 26
ring-spinning 12
Roberts, Ellen 139
rolags 11, 14, 33–36, 56, 57
  making 36, 37, 56
  woolen spinning 56, 57
rovings 14, 40, 41, 54, 55
  worsted-style 14
rubber gloves 77, 140, 140
Rumpelstiltskin 12, 13
Ryono, Naomi 134, 135, 136

**S**
S-twist 59, 64
salad spinner 30, 77
sample swatches 132
Scotch tension 18, *18*, *20*, 52, 53
scouring 14, 30
  *see also* washing
selling online 129–130
semi-woolen yarns 56
semi-worsted yarns 56, 58
short-draw technique 12
silk 24, *25*, 44, 54
silk brick 54
skein, making a 74–75
skein winder *19*, 22
Slater, Hannah (née Brown) 12
Slater, Samuel 12
Sleeping Beauty 12, *19*
slipcase, knitted 120–121
slubs
  correcting 56
  spinning a slub yarn 63
soy fiber *27*
soya "silk" 26
spindle spinning 46–49
  spinning with a bottom-whorl
    suspended spindle 46–48
  spinning with a top-whorl spindle 49
spindle wheels 10, 12
spindle whorls 10, 12
spindles 16
  anatomy of *17*
  bottom whorl *16*
  specialist *17*
  top whorl *16–17*
spinning demonstrations 12, 128, 140
spinning direction 59
spinning from the fold 58
spinning guilds 12, 14, 33, 131
spinning for a project
  accurate weighing method 132
  final check 132
  McMorran balance 133
  measured skein method 132
  record sheet 133
Spinning Jenny 12, *12*
spinning ratios 18, *18*, *19*, *20*, 52, 55, 60
squirrel cage swift *23*
static 77
steaming 77, 140
Stokes, Marianne *11*
Swett, Sarah C. 138
swift 22, *23*, 128

**T**
tassels 117–119
teaching 131
teasing 31
Tell Arpachiyah, Iraq 10
Tencel® 26, *27*
tension
  adjusting 52–53
  maintaining 48
  and weight of spindle 46
texture 62
thick spinning 60, 61
thick and thin yarns 70
thigh-spinning technique 10
thin spinning 60–61
threading hook *20*, 51
throwster's silk 24
treadle 10, *11*, 12, *20*
"true woolen" yarns 56

**U**
umbrella swift *23*

**W**
warping board 22, *23*
washing
  other yarns 77
  wool spun in the grease 77
  yarn from pre-dyed fibers 77
  *see also* scouring
website 126, *126*, *129*
Wensleydale wool *25*, 35
wheel spinning 50–53
  adjusting the tension 52–53
  attach a leader 51
  preparing for spinning 50
  sitting at a double treadle wheel 50
  sitting at a single treadle wheel 50
  starting to spin 53
wheels 18–21
  anatomy of 20, *20–21*
  Ashford Joy *18*
  Ashford Traditional *18*, *21*
  book charkha *19*
  charkha 10, *11*, *19*
  double-treadle 12, *18*, *19*
  folding 12, *18*, *19*, *20*
  Great Wheel (Walking Wheel) 10, *11*, *19*
  Lendrum wheel *19*
  Schacht Sidekick folding *19*, *20*
  single-treadle *18*, *18*
winding balls 78–79
  center-pull balls 79
  creating solid balls 78
  nostepinne method 79
  twist influence 79
wool 42, 44
  Bowmont 55
  Cormo 55
  Corriedale 60
  Merino 35, 55, 60
  washing 77
woolen spinning 14, 46, 56–57
  American long-draw spinning 56
  English long-draw spinning 57
worsted spinning 14, 40, 41, 46, 54–55
  correcting spinning thickness 55
wrapper 71, 73

**Y**
yarn gauge 22, *23*
yarns
  bouclé yarn 102–103
  bullion yarn 106–107
  cable-plied yarn 88–89
  chain-plied color yarn 98–99
  color-blended yarn 90–91
  core-spun yarns 100–101
  flecked yarn 92–93
  lustrous worsted yarn 84–85
  paper yarn 104–105
  slub yarn 94–95
  soft knitting yarn 82–83
  spiral thick and thin yarn 86–87
  three-ply chunky yarn 96–97

**Z**
Z-twist 59, 64

# Credits

Quarto would like to thank the following agencies for supplying images for inclusion in this book:

Wikipedia p.11l
National Congress Library p.11tr
Alamy p.11br
Getty Images p.12br
Art Archive p.13t
© 2011 Ashford Handicrafts Ltd p.18br
Eling Chang www.rhinofluff.com p.100–101
LAILA GRAINAWI p.126t
Ashley Marineau www.neauveau.com; www.shopneauveau.com p.127r
Riin Gill www.happyfuzzyarn.com p.128b
Naomi Ryono www.knottynaomi.etsy.com p.129l
Ellen Roberts www.shepherdsmoon.co.uk p.129r
Wendy Morris at The Handweavers Studio & Gallery p.131b

Quarto would also like to thank The Handweavers Studio & Gallery for kindly supplying tools and materials:

Wendy Morris
The Handweavers Studio & Gallery
140 Seven Sisters Road
London  N7 7NS
Tel: 020 7272 1891
www.handweavers.co.uk

All other artists are acknowleged and credited next to their work.